The Wordsworth
Dictionary of First Names

—

Iseabail Macleod and Terry Freedman

Wordsworth Reference

This edition published 1995 by Wordsworth Editions Ltd,
Cumberland House, Crib Street, Ware, Hertfordshire SG12 9ET.

Wordsworth ® is a registered trade mark of
Wordsworth Editions Ltd

Text copyright © Scaramouche Promotions Ltd 1995.
All other material copyright © Wordsworth Editions Ltd 1995.

ISBN 1-85326-366-4

Printed and bound in Great Britain
by Mackays of Chatham plc, Chatham, Kent

Introduction

A country's store of first names reflects its history, religion, literature, culture and aspirations. We have tried here to give a wide selection of names currently or recently used in Britain. Many of the common variant or familiar forms are also given, though these proliferate to such an extent and so rapidly, that it is impossible to cover them all.

The main purpose of a dictionary of first names is to provide parents with a choice of names for their children, but we offer it also as a reference for those who are simply curious about the meanings, not only of well-used names, but of those such as Pancras or Cleopatra, familiar enough, but rarely seen on birth certificates.

Many of the names still in use in Britain are Biblical in origin and have been passed down through families over the centuries. Although the practice of naming children after close relatives is less widespread, many of these old names still maintain their popularity. After the Norman Conquest, French names, many Germanic in origin, reached these shores and continue to play a part.

Celtic names, of Welsh and Gaelic origin, are found, especially in Wales, Scotland and Ireland, but some, such as Gwen, Gareth, Sheila and Kenneth, have found a wider appeal, though often in anglicized forms. Conversely, many names popular in Welsh and in Scottish and Irish Gaelic are not Celtic in origin, but altered forms of other names.

Surnames used as first names are popular; formerly they were used mainly as male names, but now increasingly, like Ashley in the USA, also as female.

Conscious of the fact that parents do not always seek the traditional names for their children, we have included newer names such as Kylie and Jade (the latter now appears in the top ten most popular girls' names), as well as names which are old but unaccountably neglected, such as Kenna.

Changing fashions are reflected in the names presented here, from the Puritan habit in the 17th century of giving as names the virtues, such as Faith, Hope and Charity, to the 19th-century vogue for flower-names which is manifested in Daisy and Iris. Novels, such as *Gone with the Wind*, have left us with a legacy of names such as Rhett, Bonnie and Scarlett. Television, film and radio have similarly had enormous influence, both with the names of their fictional characters and those of the actors and artistes themselves. Sports stars have brought such names as Ryan into the top ten boys' names.

The wish to identify with a particular cultural group comes out strongly in name fashions, so that a family's national pride may dictate Pádraig rather than Patrick. The preoccupations of cultural groups throughout the ages are traced clearly in the breakdown of the components of a name — for example the importance of the horse to the Germanic tribes is clear from the number of names containing 'hros' (horse), mistakenly associated with 'rose' in modern times. The Anglo-Saxons were evidently preoccupied with wealth and prosperity, judging by the popularity of the 'Ed-' names, such as Edward, in which 'ed-' means prosperity. All this, we hope, is food for thought for those who will use this dictionary not only to name their babies, but to gain insight into a special area of British culture.

Other forms

Forms in other languages are also included where relevant, especally from Welsh and from Scottish and Irish Gaelic. When these are present the section is headed 'Other forms' rather than 'Variant forms', even when some of the latter are included.

All other forms are given their own entries, eg

Geoff familiar form of **Geoffrey**.

except where the form follows immediately on the main form — see **Humphrey**.

Pronunciation

Pronunciation is given, but only where it is likely to present a problem, in whatever way seemed clearest in each individual case. Note the following:

The stressed syllable is marked by bold type, eg

Ida [eye-da]

The pronunciation guides to words from Welsh, Gaelic and other languages are only approximate.

-kh- = the last sound in Scottish 'loch', Welsh 'bach' or German 'ich'.

-oe- = approximately the sound in French 'oeuf' or German 'Goethe'.

Aaran variant form of **Aaron.**

Aaron (m)
Biblical, of uncertain origin. In the Old Testment (Exodus 4:7) Aaron
was the brother of Moses and used his persuasive tongue to beg the
Pharoahs to let the Israelites leave Egypt. The story of how he
miraculously turned his rod into a flowering almond tree is the
origin of plant names such as Aaron's Rod. The name is common in
the USA, as with the composer Aaron Copland.
Variant forms: **Aaran, Aron, Arron.**
Familiar forms: **Arn, Arnie.**

Abagail variant form of **Abigail.**

Abbie familiar form of **Abigail.**

Abby familiar form of **Abigail,** used as a name in its own right.

Abe familiar form of **Abraham** and **Abel.**

Abel (m)
Biblical, from Hebrew meaning 'breath'. Abel was the second son of
Adam and Eve, murdered by his jealous brother Cain. The Dutch
navigator Abel Tasman (1603-1659) was famous for his discovery of
Tasmania and New Zealand.
Familiar form: **Abe.**

Abigail (f)
Biblical, from Hebrew meaning 'father rejoices'. Abigail was one of
King David's wives. She referred to herself as his handmaid and in
consequence the name became a term for a servant in the18th
century. In the last 30 years the name has been popular.
Variant form: **Abagail.**
Familiar forms: **Abby, Abbie, Gail.**

Abner (m)
Biblical, from Hebrew meaning 'my father is light'. Abner was
related to King Saul and commanded his army. The name has been
little used this century apart from the name of the hero of the cartoon
Li'l Abner in the USA.

Other form: **Avner** (Hebrew form favoured by Jews).

Abraham (m)
Biblical, from Hebrew meaning 'father of the multitude'. Abraham was called by God to be father of the Hebrew nation. It was popular in the USA, like many Old Testament names and especially because of the president Abraham Lincoln(1809-1865), until the early 20th century.
Other form: **Abram**.
Familiar forms: **Abe, Bram.**

Abram other form of **Abraham.**

Absolom (m)
Biblical, from Hebrew meaning 'my father is peace'. Absolom was the handsome favourite son of King David, but rebelled against his father. He was caught and killed when his hair tangled in an overhanging branch and trapped him. Notable literary bearers of the name are in Dryden's *Absolom and Achitophel* and Absolon (French form) in the Miller's tale by Chaucer. The name is extremely rare in modern times.
Other form: **Axel** (Swedish).

Ad familiar form of **Adam.**

Ada familiar form of **Adelaide.**

Adam (m)
Biblical, from Hebrew meaning 'red' (referring either to the colour of earth or of human skin) from the Old Testament story of how God created Adam, the first man, from clay. The name has always been popular and famous bearers include the 18th-century economist Adam Smith.
Familiar forms: **Ad, Addie, Addy.**

Adan variant form of **Aidan.**

Addie familiar form of **Adam.**

Addy familiar form of **Adam.**

Ade familiar form of **Adrian**.

Adela familiar form of **Adelaide**.

Adelaide (f)
From Germanic *adelheit* meaning 'nobility'. Used in Britain from the eighteenth century onwards and made better known by Adelaide (1792-1849) wife of King William IV. Adelaide in Australia was called after her.
Other form: **Adèle** (French).
Familiar forms: **Ada, Adela, Della, Adelina, Adeline**; and **Heidi** (from Swiss German).

Adelia (f)
Derived from **Adela**.
Familiar form: **Delia**.

Adelina, Adeline familiar forms of Adelaide. Well-known because of Adelina Patti, the famous Italian-born soprano (1843-1919) who settled in Wales and because of the song 'Sweet Adeline'.

Aden variant form of **Aidan**.

Adie familiar form of **Aidan**.

Adina (f)
From Hebrew meaning 'desire'. Originally a male name. Uncommon, but appears in Donizetti's opera *L'Elisir d'amore* whose heroine is the fickle Adina.

Adlai (m) [ad-lay]
From Hebrew meaning 'ornament'. Rare apart from the notable example of Adlai Stevenson, an American politician in the 1960s.

Adolf variant of **Adolphus**.

Adolphus (m)
From Germanic meaning 'noble' + 'wolf'. Neither this form nor the

modern German form **Adolf** are very common since Adolf Hitler
brought the name into disrepute.
Other form: **Adolf**.
Familiar form: **Dolphus**.

Adrian (m)
From the Roman family name **Hadrianus**, meaning 'from Adria', a
city in Northern Italy, and the name of the Emperor Hadrian who
ordered the building of the fortified wall across the north of England
in 120 AD. In 1154 Nicholas Breakspear, an Englishman, became
Pope as Adrian IV. The name became popular in Britain from 1950
onwards.
Familiar forms: **Ade, Adie**.

Adrianne variant form of **Adrienne**.

Adrienne (f)
French female form of **Adrian**.
Variant form: **Adrianne**.
Familiar forms: **Drena, Drina**.

Aeneas see **Angus**.

Affery   variant form of **Aphra**.

Afra variant form of **Aphra**.

Agatha (f)
From Greek meaning 'a good woman'. It was the name of a 3rd-
century martyr. Popular in the Middle Ages, but much less popular
nowadays apart from the famous detective-story writer Agatha
Christie (1890-1976).
Familiar form: **Aggie**.

Aggie familiar form of **Agatha, Agnes**.

Agnes (f)
From Greek meaning 'pure', but from early times people have
connected it with the Latin 'agnus', meaning 'lamb', thus the symbol

of St Agnes is a lamb. She was a 4th-century Roman put to death at the age of 13 for her Christianity and her refusal to marry.
Other forms: **Agneta, Anis, Annice, Annis** and **Inez** (Spanish).
Familiar forms: **Aggie, Nessa, Nessy, Nessie** (Scottish), **Nesta** (Welsh).

Aibhilín see **Eileen**.

Aidan (m)
From Irish Gaelic **Aidán**, familiar form **Aed** meaning 'fire'. St Aidan (d. 651) came from the Isle of Iona to Christianise Northumbria and set up a monastery on the island of Lindisfarne.
Other forms: **Hayden, Haydon, Haydn** [hay-den] (all Welsh).
Variant forms: **Adan, Aden, Aiden**.
Familiar forms: **Adie, Ade**.

Aileen variant form of **Eileen**.

Ailie see **Helen**.

Ailsa (f)
From the name of the island Ailsa Craig in the Firth of Clyde. Now also used outside Scotland.

Aimée see **Amy**.

Áine (f) [awn-ye]
From Irish Gaelic meaning 'splendour', often anglicized as **Ann** or **Hannah**.

Ainie familiar form of **Ainslie**.

Ainsley (m and f)
A surname probably meaning 'meadow' or 'clearing' in Old English.
Other form: **Ainslie**.
Familiar form: **Ainie**.

Aisha (f) [eye-sha]
From Arabic meaning 'woman'. The ninth and favourite wife of the Prophet Mohammed in the 7th century. Heroine of Rider Haggard's

novel *She* where she is known as 'she who must be obeyed' (later, frequently used of Mrs Thatcher).
Variant form: **Ayesha**.

Aisling (f) [ash-ling]
From Irish Gaelic possibly meaning 'vision, dream'.
Variant form: **Aislinn**.

Aithne [eth-nee] variant form of **Eithne**.

Al familiar form of **Alan, Albert, Alexander,** and other names beginning thus.

Alan (m)
The meanings 'rock', 'harmony' and 'noble' have been suggested but the origin is uncertain. The name appeared in England after the Norman conquest with Alan, Earl of Brittany and has been popular ever since. From Chaucer with Alyn in *The Reeve's Tale* to Robert Louis Stevenson's Alan Breck in *Kidnapped* it has been regularly used in literature.
Other forms: **Allan, Allen, Ailean** (Scottish Gaelic), **Alun** (Welsh).
Familiar form: **Al**.

Alana (f)
Female form of **Alan**.
Other forms : **Alanna, Allanna, Alannah** (the last is influenced by an Irish Gaelic term of endearment, *a leanbh,* used when speaking to a child).
Familiar form: **Lana**.

Alasdair Scottish Gaelic form of **Alexander**. Alasdair Gray is a modern Scottish writer.

Alastair see **Alexander**.

Alastar Irish Gaelic form of **Alexander**.

Alaster see **Alexander**.

Alban (m)
From Latin meaning an inhabitant of Alba Longa (an area of Rome), and the name of the first British martyr, a Roman soldier living in Verulanium (later St Albans) who was put to death for sheltering a persecuted Christian priest.
Familiar forms: **Albie, Alby.**

Albert (m)
From Old English meaning 'noble' + 'bright'. Queen Victoria's marriage to Prince Albert in 1840 brought the name into prominence in Britain. Famous bearers of the name in modern times are Albert Einstein the great mathematician and physicist, and Albert Finney the actor.
Familiar forms: **Al, Bert, Bertie.**

Albie familiar form of **Alban.**

Alby familiar form of **Alban.**

Aldous (m)
From Germanic meaning 'old', rare apart from the writer Aldous Huxley (1894-1963).

Alec familiar form of **Alexander** commonly used now as an independent name.

Aled (m)
From the name of a river in North Wales. The singer Aled Jones has made the name known outside Wales.

Alena see **Madeleine.**

Alethea (f) [al-eethea].
From Greek meaning 'truth'.

Alex (m and f)
Familiar form of **Alexander** or **Alexandra,** commonly used an independent name.

Alexa familiar form of **Alexandra,** used as an independent name.

Alexander (m)
From Latin, based on Greek meaning 'defend' + 'man, warrior'.
Became widely used throughout Europe, largely because of tales and
legends about Alexander the Great, King of Macedonia in the 4th
century BC. Especially popular in Scotland, where three medieval
kings bore this name.
Other forms: **Alasdair** (Scottish Gaelic, with anglicized variants
Alastair, Alaster, Alistair), **Alastar** (Irish Gaelic).
Familiar forms: **Al, Ali, Alex, Alec, Sandy, Sandie, Lex.**

Alexandra (f)
Female form of **Alexander**, popularised by Queen Alexandra, wife of
Edward VII.
Other forms: **Alexandria, Alexandrina, Alexina.**
Familiar forms: **Alex, Alix, Alexa, Lexy, Lexie:** also **Zandra, Sandra,
Sandie, Sandy** (now often used as names in their own right),

Alexia variant form of **Alexis.**

Alexie variant form of **Alexis.**

Alexina variant form of **Alexandra.**

Alexis (m and f)
From Greek meaning 'helper' or 'defender'. More usually now a
girl's name, well-known because of Joan Collins' role in the TV series
'Dynasty'.
Variant forms: **Alexia** and **Alexie.**
Familiar forms: **Lexie, Lexy.**

Alf familiar form of **Alfred.**

Alfie familiar form of **Alfred.**

Alfred (m)
From Old English meaning 'elf counsel' or 'good counsel'. Alfred the
Great, 9th-century King of England, battled with the Vikings,
promoted education and learning and was the 'father of the British
Navy'. Alfred Hitchcock (1899-1980) was a famous film maker.

Familiar forms: **Alf, Alfie, Fred**.

Alfreda (f)
Female form of Alfred.

Algernon (m)
From Norman-French meaning 'with a moustache' and probably a
nickname for someone who (unusually amongst the Normans) was
wearing one.
Familiar form: **Algie**.

Ali variant form of **Alexander** or **Alice**.

Alice (f)
From Germanic meaning 'nobility'. Lewis Carroll immortalized the
name in *Alice in Wonderland*.
Other forms: **Alison, Alys** (Welsh).
Familiar forms: **Allie, Ali**.

Alistair see **Alexander**.

Alix familiar form of **Alexandra**.

Allan variant form of **Alan**.

Allanna variant form of **Alana**.

Allegra (f)
From Italian meaning 'joyful, cheerful', and given as a name to his
daughter by the poet Lord Byron.

Allen variant form of **Alan**.

Allie variant form of **Alice**.

Alma (f)
Three possible origins are: from Latin meaning 'kind or caring', as in
Alma Mater meaning one's old school or college, or from Italian 'soul'
or from Hebrew 'maiden'. After the battle of Alma (1854) in the
Crimean War, it was popular in Britain.

Almira (f)
From Arabic meaning 'princess'.

Aloysius (m) [al-o-wish-us]
A Latin form of **Louis**. St Aloysius (1568-1591) was the patron saint of youth and students. A noble, he renounced his title, became a missionary and died of the plague in Rome.

Althea (f)
From Greek meaning 'good or 'wholesome'.

Alun Welsh form of **Alan.**

Alvar (m)
From Old English meaning 'elf warrior'

Alvin (m)
From Old English meaning 'elf' + 'friend'.

Alys Welsh form of **Alice.**

Amabel (f)
From Latin meaning 'lovable'.
Other forms: **Mabel, Annabel.**

Amanda (f)
From Latin meaning 'to be loved' or 'lovable' and consistently popular since the 18th century.
Familiar forms: **Mandy, Mandi.**

Amber (f)
From the name of the gem; made famous by the 20th-century romantic novel *Forever Amber* (1944) by Kathleen Winsor.

Ambrose (m)
From Greek meaning 'divine'. The 4th-century bishop of Milan, St Ambrose, made the name venerable.
Other form: **Emrys** (Welsh).

Amelia (f)
Partly from the same root as **Emily** but also from Germanic names containing the element *Amal* meaning 'work'. It is the name of the novel *Amelia* (1751) by English Novelist Henry Fielding.
Variant form: **Emilia**

Amhlaigh see **Olave.**

Amhlaoibh see **Humphrey.**

Amos (m)
Biblical, from Hebrew meaning 'strong'. The Old Testament prophet, Amos, was a herdsman who denounced the sinful ways of the people of Israel. He was the first prophet to have a book of the Bible named after him.

Amy (f)
From French **Aimée** meaning 'beloved'. Popular especially since the end of the 19th century. It is the name of the heroines in *Little Dorrit* by Charles Dickens and in *Little Women* by Louisa M Alcott.

Anabel variant form of **Annabel.**

Anastasia (f)
From Greek meaning 'resurrection'. A famous name because of the (false) claims of a woman to be Princess Anastasia, the daughter of the Czar Nicholas of Russia, killed with the rest of the Russian royal family in the Revolution (1917).
Familiar forms: **Stacey, Stacie, Stacy** which have a popularity far in excess of the original name.

Anders Scandinavian form of **Andrew.**

André see **Andrew.**

Andrea (f)
Female form of **Andrew.**

Andrew (m)
From Greek meaning 'manly'. St Andrew, one of the twelves

apostles, converted by St John the Baptist, was crucified in Greece. He is the patron saint of Scotland and because his cross was said to have been x-shaped, the Scottish flag takes that form. The name has always been well-liked.
Familiar forms: **Andy, Drew.**
Other forms: **Anders** (Scandinavian), **André** (French).

Aneirin variant form of **Aneurin.**

Aneurin (m) [an-eye-rin]
Thought to be a Welsh form of the Latin **Honorius.** Famous in Wales because of the 6th-century poet whose name is spelt **Aneirin** and also because of the Labour minister Aneurin Bevan (1897-1960).
Variant form: **Aneirin.**
Familiar form: **Nye.**

Angel (m)
From Greek meaning 'messenger, angel'. Little used in Protestant countries, possibly owing to Puritan doubts about the desirablility of using it as a name, but popular in Catholic countries. Thomas Hardy's character Angel Clare in *Tess of the D'Urbervilles* is one of the few examples in English literature.

Angela (f)
From Greek meaning 'messenger or angel'. Consistently used in Britain from the 19th century onwards.
Variant forms: **Angeline, Angelina.**
Familiar form: **Angie.**

Angelica (f)
From Latin meaning 'angelic'.

Angelina variant form of **Angela.**

Angeline variant form of **Angela.**

Angharad (f) [ank-har-ad]
From Welsh meaning 'beloved'.

Angie familiar form of **Angela, Angelina.**

Angus (m)
From Scottish Gaelic **Aonghas**, probably meaning 'one' + 'choice'. It is sometimes anglicized as **Aeneas** (both pronounced [oe-nas]).

Anika (f)
Usually taken to be a variant of **Anneka** but in this spelling could be from a Hausa word meaning 'sweet face', which would explain its use among slaves in the 18th century.

Anis variant form of **Agnes.**

Anita (f)
Originally the Spanish familiar form of **Ann**, but frequently used as an independent name, epecially in the USA as in Anita Loos, author of *Gentlemen Prefer Blondes* and the actress Anita Ekberg.

Ann (f)
An English form of Hebrew **Hannah**. In various forms, the name has always been popular in the English-speaking world, probably because the Virgin Mary's mother was Anna. It is frequently combined with other names or used as a middle name. It is a royal name, a frequent literary name, the name of Shakespeare's wife, of the writer of *The Diary of Anne Frank*. See also **Áine.**
Other forms: **Anna, Anne, Anneka, Annika** (both Swedish), **Anita.** See also **Anya.**
Familiar forms: **Annie, Nan, Nannie, Nancy, Nina.**

Anna variant of **Ann**, being the Latin form of **Hannah.**

Annabel (f)
Of obscure origin, possibly simply **Anna + Belle,** or it may be a variant of **Amabel.** Popular in Scotland, it has been used in the Scottish Highlands as an anglicization of the Gaelic **Barabal** (which comes from the same Greek root as **Barbara**).
Other forms: **Annabella, Annabelle, Anabel.**

Annalisa (f)
An English form of the German **Annaliese** which is a combination of **Anna** and **Liese** (Elizabeth).

Anne variant form of **Ann.**

Anneka (f)
Swedish form of **Ann.**
Variant form: **Annika.**

Annetta variant form of **Annette.**

Annette (f)
Diminutive of Ann, used as a name in its own right.
Variant form: **Annetta.**
Familiar forms: **Netta, Netty, Nettie.**

Annice (f)
From Greek meaning 'fulfilment'.

Annie familiar form of **Ann.**

Annika variant form of **Anneka.**

Annwyl (f) [an-well]
From Welsh meaning 'beloved'.

Anona (f)
Possibly from Latin meaning 'pineapple' but may be from the Roman goddess Annona. The name was highlighted by the fame of Anona Wynn, radio quiz personality in the 1950s.

Anraoi Irish Gaelic form of **Henry.**

Anselm (m)
From Germanic meaning 'divine helmet'. St Anselm was an 11th-century Archbishop of Canterbury and a follower of St Augustine's teaching.

Anselma (f)
Female form of **Anselm,** not common.
Familiar forms: **Selma** and **Zelma** are used as independent names, and are more popular than the original.

Anthea (f)
From Greek meaning 'flowery', sometimes used to mean the goddess of spring.

Anthony (m)
The more usual written form of **Antony**. Both are pronounced in the same way in Britain but in the USA the '-th-' is pronounced as in *thin*. The 'h' was introduced under the mistaken belief that it derived from *anthos*, Greek for 'flower'. It derives from the ancient Roman family name **Antonius** of obscure but probably Etruscan origin. See also **Antony**.

Antoine French form of **Antony**.

Antoinette (f)
Female form of **Antoine** .The fame of Queen Marie Antoinette, executed in the French Revolution, has made the name unforgettable.

Anton (m)
German and Russian form of **Antony**.

Antonia (f)
Female form of **Antony**, popular in the 20th century. Antonia Fraser is a historical writer.
Familiar form: **Tony, Toni.**

Antony (m)
From the Roman family name **Antonius**. This spelling, without 'h' is the historically correct version.The best- known member was Marcus Antonius, fellow Consul of Julius Caesar in ancient Rome. St Antony the Great and St Antony of Padua gave the name prestige and many modern bearers of the name are well known in the theatre (Antony Quinn) and literature (Antony Powell).
Other forms: **Anthony, Antoine** (French), **Anton** (German and Russian). See also **Anthony**.
Familiar form: **Tony.**

Anwen (f) [an-wen]
From Welsh meaning 'very beautiful'.

Anya (f)
Anglicized spelling of the Spanish form of **Anna**.

Aodh see **Hugh**.

Aonghas see **Angus**.

Aphra (f)
From Hebrew meaning 'dust'. Aphra Behn (1644–89) was probably
the first professional woman writer in Britain, author of comedies;
also spy and adventuress. Dickens uses the alternative spelling for
his Affery Flintwich in *Little Dorrit*.
Variant forms: **Affery** and **Afra**.

April (f)
Came into use this century and was equated with **Averil** which was
popularly interpreted as a form of **Avril**, the French name of the
fourth month. In fact, **Averil** is derived from the name of St Everild, a
7th-century saint.

Arabella (f)
From Latin meaning 'obliging' or it may be a form of **Amabel**.
Arabella Fermor was immortalized by Alexander Pope when in 1712
he published his *Rape of the Lock*, a satire based on an incident in
which Lord Petrie stole a lock of Arabella's hair.

Arailt Scottish Gaelic form of **Harold**.

Araminta (f)
A name invented by the playwright Sir John Vanbrugh for his play
The Confederacy in 1705. (Probably modelled on the *Aminta* by the
Italian poet Tasso.)

Aranrhod (f) [ar-an-throd]
From Welsh meaning 'silver' + 'coin, wheel'.
Variant form: **Arianrhod** [a-ree-an-throd].

Archbold variant form of **Archibald**.

Archibald (m)
From Germanic meaning 'noble' + 'bold'. It was introduced into
Britain by the Normans and became popular in Scotland through a
mistaken association with 'archbishop'. The name was seen as an
English version of the Gaelic **Gilleasbaig** (see **Gillespie**) meaning
'servant of the bishop'. It was a favourite name of the Douglas and
Campbell clans.
Variant form: **Archbold.**
Familiar forms: **Archie, Archy.**

Areta other form of **Aretha.**

Aretha (f)
From Greek meaning 'virtue'. Aretha Franklin is an American Blues
singer.
Other form: **Areta.**

Arfon (m)
From Welsh meaning 'facing Anglesea'.

Ariadne (f)
Possibly from Greek meaning 'holy, sacred'. In the Greek myth,
Ariadne was the princess who helped Theseus to escape from the
labyrinth where he had been imprisoned by her father King Minos
and doomed to be killed by the monstrous minotaur.

Ariane French form of **Ariadne.**

Arianrhod variant form of **Aranrhod.**

Arianwen (f) [a-ree-an-wen]
From Welsh meaning 'silver' + 'fair, blessed'.

Arlene variant form of **Arline** and now the preferred form.

Arletta variant form of **Arlette.**

Arlette (f)
A French name which appeared in Britain after World War II,
probably derived from the familiar form of **Charlotte.**

Variant form: **Arletta**.
Familiar form: **Lettie, Letty**.

Arline (f)
Possibly derived from the Hungarian Karolina. The heroine of Balfe's opera, *The Bohemian Girl* is the first record of this name and may be connected with the name of his wife Lina, short for Karolina.
Variant form: **Arlene**.

Arn familiar form of **Aaron, Arnold**.

Arnie familiar form of **Aaron, Arnold**.

Arnold (m)
From Norman-French of Germanic origin meaning 'strength of the eagle'. An apt name for the film star and strongman Arnold Schwarzenegger.
Familiar forms: **Arn, Arnie**.

Aron variant of **Aaron**.

Arron variant of **Aaron**.

Art familiar form of **Arthur**.

Arthur (m)
The name's origin is in doubt; it is first found in the Latin form **Artorius**. It is forever associated with the legends of King Arthur, the 6th-century hero said to have championed the British tribes against the Saxon invaders. He is thought by some to buried at Glastonbury. His adventures gave rise to the stories of the Knights of the Round Table. The name has been well used, and famous bearers include the Duke of Wellington.
Familiar form: **Art**. Art Garfunkel is an American singer/songwriter.

Asa (m) [ay-za]
From Hebrew meaning 'physician'. Asa Briggs is the name of a famous historian (1921-).

Ash familiar form of **Ashley**.

Ashleigh variant form of **Ashley.**

Ashley (m and f)
From the surname, itself from many place names meaning 'ash wood'. Originally a common place name and surname but has been a first name for over a century, increasingly popular as a female name in the USA. As a male name it became well-known as a result of the book and film of Margaret Mitchell's *Gone with the Wind*.
Variant forms: **Ashleigh, Ashlie.**
Familiar form: **Ash.**

Astrid (f)
From Old Norse meaning 'divine beauty'. It has become well known as the name of a Queen of the Belgians.

Atara (f) [at-ah-ra]
Biblical, from Hebrew meaning 'crown'. In the Old Testament, Atara was one of Jerahmeel's wives (I Chronicles 2:26).

Athene (f) [ath-ee-nee]
From Greek after the goddess of wisdom. Athene Zyler is a well known actress.

Athol (m and f)
From the surname, itself from the Scottish place name, which may be from Gaelic meaning 'new Ireland'. Usually a male name, but occasionally used for females.
Variant form: **Atholl, Athole.**

Auberon (m)
From Germanic meaning 'noble' or 'bear-like' or, others believe, from the name **Aubrey**. Uncommon apart from Auberon Waugh (1934-), writer and journalist.
Variant form: **Oberon**, the Fairy King in *A Midsummer Night's Dream*.

Aubrey (m)
From Germanic meaning 'elf counsel'. Sometimes used by Jews as an English form of **Abraham**. Aubrey Beardsley(1872-1898) was a popular illustrator.

Audrey (f)
Colloquial pronunciation of the name **Etheldreda**, from Old English meaning 'noble strength', resulted in the form 'Audrey' which in turn gave the adjective 'tawdry' to the language because of the poor quality goods sold at St Audrey's fairs. St Etheldreda, that is St Audrey, was a 7th-century princess who founded a monastery at Ely and was famed as a virgin saint despite two marriages.

Augusta (f)
From Latin meaning 'venerable'. It was the name of the sister of the poet Lord Byron.
Familiar forms: **Gus, Gussie.**

Augustin variant form of **Augustine.**

Augustine (m)
From a diminutive form of **Augustus**. St Augustine of Hippo (354-430) was a north African pagan who was converted to Christianity in Rome and became a bishop and an influential thinker and writer.
Variant forms: **Augustin, Austen, Austin.**

Augustus (m)
From the Latin meaning 'venerable'. It was the name of Roman emperors.
Familiar forms: **Gus** and **Gussie.**

Aulay Scottish form of **Olave.**

Aurelia (f)
From the Roman family name **Aurelius** derived from Latin meaning 'gold'.

Auriel (f)
From Latin meaing 'golden'.
Other forms: **Auriol** and **Auriole.**

Aurora (f)
From the Latin name of the Roman goddess of the dawn. Mainly used in poetry, as in Elizabeth Barret Browning`s *Aurora Leigh* (1856).

Austen variant of **Augustine**.

Austin variant of **Augustine**.

Ava (f) [ay-va, ah-va]
In addition to being a familiar form of **Gustava**, this can be another
form of Eva , reflecting the way Eva is pronounced in many
European countries. Ava Gardner, film star in the 1940s, popularized
the name, though her name tended to be pronounced to rhyme with
Java.

Aveline (f)
From Norman-French of Germanic origin. Ultimately derived from
Avis.

Averil (f) [av-ril]
A form of the name of the 7th-century Saint Everild whose name
derives from Old English words meaning 'boar' + 'fight'.
Other form: **Avril**, sometimes taken to be the French for April.

Avis (f)
From a Roman family name **Avitius**, but also often taken to be from
the Latin *avis* meaning 'bird'.

Avner Hebrew form of **Abner**.

Avril see **April, Averil**.

Axel (m)
A Scandinavian form of **Absolom** made famous by the author Axel
Munthe who described his life on the Isle of Capri in *San Michele*
(1929).

Ayesha variant form of **Aisha**.

Azariah (m) [a-zar-ee-ah]
From Hebrew meaning 'Jehovah has helped'. A rare name in modern
times, but brought to public attention in the 1982 Australian case of a

mother accused of murdering her child called Azaria (unusually for a girl). The mother was later exonerated.

Babs familiar form of **Barbara**.

Barabal see **Annabel**.

Barb familiar form of **Barbara**.

Barbara (f)
From Latin derived from Greek meaning 'foreign woman'. St Barbara was a 3rd-century saint whose great beauty caused her father to imprison her in a tower away from all men, but when she became a Christian he beheaded her. He in turn was struck by lightning as a punishment from God. Always popular, the name has become more so in the 20th century.
Variant form: **Barbra**.
Familiar forms: **Babs, Barb, Barbie**.
Barbie familiar form of **Barbara**, name of a widely used toy, the Barbie doll.

Barbra variant form of **Barbara**, as in the name of the American singer, Barbra Streisand.

Barnabas (m)
From Hebrew meaning 'son of encouragement'. In the New Testament the companion of St Paul bore this name.
Other form: **Barnaby**, much preferred to the original.
Familiar form: **Barnie, Barney, Barny**.

Barnard variant form of **Bernard**.

Barney, Barnie, Barny familiar forms of **Barnard, Barnabas**. Barny Rubble is a cartoon character of the 1990s.

Baron (m)
A surname (from the title) used as a first name.
Variant form: **Barron**.

Barrie (m)
Sometimes taken to be a variant of **Barry**, but likely to be from the
surname (derived from Scottish and Welsh place names), as in Sir
James Barrie, author of *Peter Pan*.

Barrfind see Barry.

Barrington (m).
From the Somerset surname, itself from various place names, derived
from an Old English personal name + 'settlement'.
Familiar form: **Barry.**

Barron variant form of Baron.

Barry (m)
From Irish Gaelic **Bairre, Barre,** familiar forms of **Fionbharr** or
Barrfind both meaning 'fair haired'. Also a common Irish surname.
Barry Island in Wales is called after a hermit who lived there.

Bart familiar form of Bartholomew.

Bartholomew (m)
Biblical from Hebrew meaning 'son of Talmai'.
Other forms: **Bartle, Bartlet.**
Familiar forms: **Bart, Bartie, Barty.**

Bartie familiar form of Bartholomew.

Barton (m)
From the surname, itself from a place name meaning 'barley' +
'settlement'.

Barty familiar form of Bartholomew.

Basil (m)
From Greek meaning 'king'. The name of Byzantine emperors and of
the Great St Basil, 4th-century Bishop of Caesarea, who attacked
heresy and improved monastic standards. More popular in Eastern
Europe, but Sir Basil Spence, Scottish architect (1907-1976), and Basil
Rathbone, actor are modern Western examples.

Bathsheba (f)
Biblical, from Hebrew meaning 'daughter of wealth'. Bathsheba, wife of Uriah, was later the lover, then wife of King David. Little used in modern times.
Familiar form: **Sheba**.

Bea familiar form of **Beatrice**.

Beatrice (f)
From Latin meaning 'one who brings blessings or happiness'. Made immortal in Dante's *Divine Comedy* in which Beatrice guides the poet through Paradise. A modern bearer was Beatrice Webb (1858-1943), social reformer with her husband Sidney.
Other form: **Beatrix**, as in Beatrix Potter (1866-1943) writer and illustrator of children's books, such as *The Tale of Peter Rabbit*.
Familiar forms: **Bea, Beattie,Trixie**.

Beavis variant form of **Bevis**.

Becky (f)
Familiar form of **Rebecca** used as a name in its own right. Literary Beckys are found in *Tom Sawyer* by Mark Twain and in *Vanity Fair* by Thackeray.

Bede (m)
From Old English meaning 'prayer'. The Venerable Bede (672-735) of Durham was the great Anglo-Saxon scholar and saint who, amongst other works, wrote the *Ecclesiastical History of the English People*.

Bel familiar form of **Belinda** and of other names containing 'bell', 'bella', 'belle'. Bel Mooney is a 20th-century writer.

Belinda (f)
Possibly from Germanic meaning 'serpent'.
Familiar forms: **Bel, Bindy, Linda, Lindy**.

Bella (f)
Italian form of the French **Belle** meaning 'beautiful', but also from familiar forms of names like **Isabella**.

Belle (f)
From French meaning 'beautiful'; also used as a familiar form of names containing 'bell', 'bella', 'belle'.

Ben familiar form of **Benjamin, Benedict** often used as a name in its own right.

Benedict (m)
From Latin meaning 'blessed'. St Benedict was a 5th-century Italian saint who founded the Benedictine order of monks.
Familiar form: **Ben.**

Benjamin (m)
Biblical, from Hebrew meaning 'son of my right hand'. Benjamin was the youngest son of Rachel and Jacob. Benjamin Franklyn (1706-1790) was an American statesman and scientist. Benjamin Disraeli (1804-1881) was a British statesman and novelist.
Familiar forms: **Ben, Benjie, Benny.**

Bentley (m)
From the surname based on a place name meaning 'place of coarse grass'. Bentley Drummle is a handsome villain in *Great Expectations* by Charles Dickens.

Berenice (f)
From Greek meaning 'one who brings victory'.
Variant form: **Bernice**, as in the writer Bernice Reubens.

Bernadette (f)
Female form of **Bernard**. The name is revered by Catholics because of St Bernardette, the French peasant girl to whom the Virgin Mary is said to have appeared at Lourdes which then became a place of pilgrimage for the sick.

Bernard (m)
From Germanic meaning 'strength of the bear'. This is the name of several saints, including the 'Apostle of the Alps' who in the 10th century, established hospices and had dogs trained (hence St Bernard

dogs) to help snowbound travellers. Many famous people have borne this name, notably George Bernard Shaw.
Variant form: **Barnard**.
Familiar form: **Bernie**.

Bernice variant form of **Berenice**.

Bernie familiar form of **Bernard**.

Bert familiar form of **Albert** and of other names ending thus; and also of **Bertram**.

Bertha (f)
From Germanic meaning 'bright'. Popular in the 19th century, but now in decline.

Bertie familiar form of **Albert** and of other names ending thus; and also of **Bertram, Bertrand**.

Bertram (m)
From Germanic meaning 'bright raven'. Common until the start of the 20th century. Bertram is the Count of Rousillon in Shakespeare's *All's Well that Ends Well*.
Familiar forms: **Bert, Bertie**.

Bertrand (m)
Possibly a French form of **Bertram**. Not common, but an outstanding bearer of the name was the philosopher, Bertrand Russell (1872-1970).
Familiar forms: **Bert, Bertie**.

Beryl (f)
From the Latin name of a mineral, beryl, one form of which produces emeralds. Often used earlier this century with other jewel names. Beryl Cook is a Plymouth painter of highly individual humorous pictures and illustrations.

Bess (f)
Originally a familiar form of **Elizabeth** often used as a name in its own right especially in the past. Bess of Hardwick in Derbyshire,

later Countess of Shrewsbury, was a famous 'iron lady' of the 16th century, known for her architectural innovation and as gaoler of Mary Queen of Scots.
Familiar forms: **Bessie, Bessy**.

Bet familiar form of **Elizabeth**.

Beth (f)
Familiar form of **Elizabeth** and of **Bethany** currently favoured and often used as a name in its own right.

Bethany (f)
The first syllable comes from Hebrew meaning 'house' and Bethany is a place name in Israel.
Familiar form: **Beth**.

Betsey familiar form of **Elizabeth**.

Betsy familiar form of **Elizabeth** favoured in the last century. Betsy Trotwood was the hero's aunt in *David Copperfield* by Charles Dickens

Bette familiar form of **Elizabeth**, not common apart from the famous film stars Bette Davis and Bette Middler.

Bettina (f)
Diminutive of **Elisabetta**, the Italian form of **Elizabeth**.

Betty familiar form of **Elizabeth**, often used as a name in its own right with enormous popularity at times, though not recently. Betty Grable was a famous film star in the 1940s.

Bev familiar form of **Beverley, Bevan , Bevis**.

Bevan (m)
From a Welsh surname ap Evan 'son of Evan'; (in Welsh names the final 'p' is often linked to the beginning of the name).
Familiar form: **Bev**.

Beverley (m and f)
From the surname, itself from a place name in East Yorkshire from

Old English meaning 'beaver' + 'meadow'. At the height of its popularity in the fifties, Beverley Nichols was the pen name of a journalist and novelist of the time.
Variant form: **Beverly** (perhaps influenced by the film suburb of Los Angeles).
Familiar form: **Bev.**

Bevis (m)
Possibly from Old French meaning 'dear son' or from a French place name. Bevis was the hero of a novel by Richard Jefferies (1882). Beavis and Butthead are cult TV animated characters.
Variant form: **Beavis.**
Familiar form: **Bev.**

Bianca (f)
From Italian meaning white. In Shakespeare's *Taming of the Shrew* Bianca is the sweet-tempered sister of the stormy Kate.

Biddy familiar form of **Bridget.**

Bill (m)
Familiar form of **William** frequently used as a name in its own right.

Billie (m and f)
A familiar form of **William** and also a female name this century. Billie Holiday (1915-1959) was a world famous American Jazz singer with an influential style of singing. The name of the tennis player, Billie-Jean King, is an example of how the name is often combined with others.

Billy familiar form of **William.**

Bindy familiar form of **Belinda.**

Bing (m)
From the nickname of Harry Crosby (1904-1977), who as Bing Crosby made his name as a crooner and film star.

Blair (m)
From the Scottish surname, itself from a place name, from Gaelic

meaning a 'flat piece of land'. Blair Peach was killed by police who were attempting to break up a demonstration in London (1979).

Blaise (m)
From Latin meaning 'crippled'. The 3rd-century martyr was an Armenian and said to help sufferers from diseases of the throat.

Blake (m)
From the surname. It is uncertain whether it comes from a word meaning 'pale' or, on the contrary, from a word meaning 'black' in Old English.

Blanche (f) [blonsh or blansh]
From French meaning 'white', popular in 19th-century America.

Blod familiar form of **Blodwen, Blodwedd.**

Blodwedd (f) [blod-wed]
From Welsh meaning 'flower face'. In Welsh myth, Blodwedd was created from flowers, but in later life was turned into an owl as a punishment for murdering her husband.
Familiar form: **Blod.**

Blodwen (f) [blod-wen]
From Welsh meaning ' blossom'. Common in Wales in the last hundred years.
Familiar form: **Blod.**

Bluebell (f)
From the name of the flower, less used than many of the flower names, but sometimes given as a second name in country areas.

Boaz (m)
From Hebrew meaning 'man of strength'. A Puritan name used in 19th-century America.

Bob familiar form of **Robert.**

Bobbie familiar form of **Robert** and **Roberta.**

Bobby familiar form of **Robert** and **Roberta**.

Bonar (m)
From the surname, itself from Old French meaning 'courteous'.
Andrew Bonar Law (1858-1923) was a British Prime Minister.

Boniface (m)
From Latin meaning 'destined for good fortune'. The name of several
Popes including Boniface VIII (1235-1303), famous for his captivity
and the enforced exile of the papacy in France.

Bonita (f)
From Spanish meaning 'pretty'.

Bonnie (f)
From a Scots word meaning 'beautiful, fine'. In *Gone with the Wind*,
(1939), by Margaret Mitchell, Scarlett O'Hara gives it to her daughter
as a pet name. The 1960s American film *Bonnie and Clyde* about two
glamorized criminals kept the name in the public mind.

Boris (m)
From Old Slavonic meaning 'battle'. Not common in the English-
speaking world but known as the name of Russian Czars, and
recently of the President, Boris Yeltsin. Boris Pasternak became
internationally famous in 1958 when his novels were translated from
Russian into English. The film star Boris Karloff played in horror
films.

Boyce (m)
From the surname, itself from numerous place names, deriving from
Old French meaning 'wood'.

Boyd (m)
From the Scottish surname, itself from Scottish Gaelic, possibly
meaning 'from the Island of Bute' (in the Firth of Clyde).

Brad (m)
Familiar form of **Bradford** and **Bradley**, increasingly popular as a
name in its own right. Brad Pitt is a young film star of the 1990s.

Bradford (m)
From the surname, itself from a place name meaning 'broad ford' in
Old English.
Familiar form: **Brad**.

Bradley (m)
From the surname, itself from a place name meaning 'broad clearing'.
Bradley Headstone is the lover of Lizzie Hexam in *Our Mutual Friend*
by Charles Dickens.
Familiar form: **Brad**.

Bram familiar form of **Abraham**. Bram Stoker (1847-1912) wrote
Dracula.

Bramwell (m)
From the Derbyshire surname meaning 'place of brambles'. William
Bramwell Booth was a General of the Salvation Army.
Other form: **Branwell**. Patrick Branwell Brontë was the feckless
brother of the novelists, Emily, Charlotte and Anne.

Brandon (m)
From the surname, itself from a place name meaning 'gorse' + 'hill'.
Variant form: **Branton**.

Branton (m)
From the surname itself from a place name meaning 'gorse' +
'settlement'. It is also a variant form of **Brandon**.

Branwell variant form of **Bramwell**.

Branwen (f)
From Welsh meaning 'raven' + 'blessed'. In Welsh myth, Branwen
was a famous beauty who caused conflict between her brother and
her husband, who was King of Ireland.

Breandán Irish Gaelic form of **Brendan**.

Breeda English form of Irish Gaelic **Bríd**. See **Bridget**.

Brenda (f)
From Old Norse meaning 'sword'. Widely used.

Brendan (m)
From Irish Gaelic probably from Welsh meaning 'prince'. It was the
name of a 6th-century saint known for founding monasteries and for
his voyages in the north Altlantic. A popular name in Ireland.
Brendan Behan (1923-1964) was a playwright and one-time member
of the IRA.
Other form: **Breandán** (Irish Gaelic).

Bret variant form of **Brett.**

Brett (m)
From Latin meaning 'Briton'.
Variant form: **Bret,** as in Bret Harte, the 19th-century writer.

Brian (m)
Originally a surname introduced to the north of England from
Ireland and to the south from Brittany. It may also come from the
Irish Gaelic meaning 'hill' or 'high, noble'. Brian Boru was a famous
11th-century king of Ireland. Popular throughout the English-
speaking world.
Variant forms: **Brien, Bryan.**

Bríd Irish Gaelic form of **Bridget.**
Brid Irish Gaelic form of **Bridget**

Bride English form of Irish Gaelic **Bríd.** (See **Bridget**).

Bridget (f)
From Irish Gaelic **Bríd,** Old Irish **Brigit** meaning 'strength'. It is the
name of a 6th-century Irish saint, the Great St Bride or Briget.
Daughter of an Ulster prince, she became a nun and founded four
monasteries.
Other forms: **Brigid, Bríd** (Irish Gaelic [breedj], **Breeda, Bride.**
Familiar forms: **Biddy** and **Bridie.**

Brien variant form of **Brian.**

Brigid variant form of **Bridget.**

Briony variant form of **Bryony**.

Bron familiar form of **Bronwen.**

Bronwen (f)
From Welsh meaning 'fair white breast'.
Familiar form: **Bron.**

Brook (f)
From the word 'brook'. Gradually coming into fashion in the 1990s, probably influenced by the actress Brook Shields.

Bruce (m)
From the Scottish surname, originally **de Brus,** borne by a noble Anglo-Norman family in medieval Scotland. King Robert I (1274-1329), known as Robert the Bruce, led the Scots to victory over the English forces at Bannockburn (1314). The name is now used throughout the English-speaking world and has become very popular in Australia.
Variant form: **Brus.**

Bruno (m)
From Germanic meaning 'bear-like'. St Bruno founded the order of Carthusian monks in the 11th century.

Brus variant form of **Bruce.**

Bryan variant form of **Brian.**

Brychan (m) [bri-khan]
From Welsh meaning 'speckled'.

Bryn (m)
From Welsh meaning 'hill'.

Brynmor (m) [brin-mor]
From Welsh meaning 'big hill'.

Bryony (f)
From the name of the climbing plant.
Other form: **Briony**.

Bud (m)
From baby pronunciation of 'brother'. Mainly used in the USA.
Other form: **Buddy**. Buddy Holly (1936-1959) was a pioneering
singer, songwriter and guitarist who has influenced rock and roll
music.

Buntie variant form of **Bunty**.

Bunty (f)
From a nickname of uncertain origin, now used as a name in its own
right. Traditionally it is the name for a pet lamb.
Variant form: **Buntie**.

Cadfael (m) [cad-fel]
From Welsh meaning 'battle' + ' metal'. Brother Cadfael is the monk
detective who is the hero of a series of novels by Ellis Peters.

Cadwallader (m)
From Welsh meaning 'leader in battle'.

Caerwyn (m) [ker-win]
From Welsh meaning 'fortress' + 'white'.

Caesar (m)
From Latin, probably meaning 'head of hair' and the family name of
Julius Caesar (102-44 BC) .It came to be the title of any Roman
emperor. It is sometimes used by families of Caribbean origin.
Variant form: **Cesar**.

Cailean see **Colin**.

Caitlín Gaelic form of **Catherine**.

Caius (m) [guy-us]
A Roman first name meaning 'rejoice'. As used in the name of

Gonville and Caius College, Cambridge, the name is pronounced [keys].
Familiar forms: **Kai** (Welsh), **Kay.**

Cal familiar form of **Cathal.**

Caleb (m)
Biblical, from Hebrew meaning 'fearless'. In the Old Testament Caleb was one of the twelve men first sent by Moses into the promised land (Numbers 26:65).

Callum, Calum see Malcolm.

Calvin (m)
From Latin meaning 'bald'. Used as a first name by Protestants in northern Europe after John Calvin, the 16th-century Reformation theologian.

Cameron (m)
From the Scottish surname, itself from Scottish Gaelic meaning 'crooked nose.'It is the name of a clan.

Camilla (f)
From a Latin first name. Fanny Burney wrote the novel *Camilla* in the 18th century. As the girl friend of Prince Charles, Camilla Parker Bowles has kept the name in the public eye.
Other form: **Camille** (French).
Familiar forms: **Cammie, Milly, Millie.**

Campbell (m)
From the Scottish surname, itself from Scottish Gaelic meaning 'crooked mouth'. It is the name of the clan.

Candace variant form of **Candice.**

Candice (f)
A title of the Queens of Ethiopia.
Variant form: **Candace.**
Familiar form: **Candy**

Caoimhínn see **Kevin.**

Cara (f)
From Latin meaning 'dear'.
Variant form: **Kara.**
Other forms: **Carine** (French), **Carina.**

Caradoc variant form of **Caradog.**

Caradog (m)
From Welsh meaning 'dear ' or 'love'. Caradog was a chieftain of the
Britons who fought against the Romans and was captured. His name
was Latinized to Caractacus.
Variant form: **Caradoc.** Caradoc Evans was (1878-1945) a Welsh
writer and harsh critic of Welsh society.

Carina variant form of **Cara.**

Carine French form of **Cara.**

Carl (m)
From Old English meaning 'a man' which is also the origin of the
name **Charles.**
Variant form: **Karl** (German).

Carla (f)
Feminine form of **Charles.** Increasingly popular since the 1950s,
Carla Lane is a successful scriptwriter for many TV soap operas.
Familiar form: **Carly, Carlie.**

Carmel (f)
The name of a mountain in Israel near Haifa. As the place was
associated with legends of the Virgin Mary, the Carmelite order was
founded there.
Other form: **Carmen.**

Carmen (f)
Although originally a variant of **Carmel** (the Spanish form), it is
thought of as a separate name and considered to be from the Latin
word meaning 'song'. The heroine of Bizet's opera *Carmen*, a

beautiful gypsy, is unfaithful to her lover, Don José, and eventually kills him.

Caro familiar form of **Carol** and **Caroline.**

Carol (m and f)
The male name can be derived from various forms of **Charles** and **Carl** or from the Irish **Cathal**. The female name, much more common, was a short form of **Caroline** but is now independent of it. For many people it has associations with Christmas carols.
Other forms: **Carroll** (m), **Carole, Carola, Caryl** (all f),
Familiar forms: **Carrie, Caro.**

Carolina Italian form of **Caroline.**

Caroline (f)
Female form of **Charles**, it became popular from when Caroline of Anspach (1683-1737) married George II and it has remained a common name.
Variant form: **Carolyn.**
Familiar forms: **Carrie, Caro.**

Caron (f)
Welsh saint's name of recent popularity and possibly thought of as a Welsh form of **Karen.**

Carren variant form of **Karen.**

Carrie (f)
Familiar form of **Carol** and **Caroline**, used as a name in its own right.
Carrie Fisher is a writer and film star.

Carroll variant form of **Carol.**

Cary (m)
From the surname, itself from the place name, made famous as a first name by the film star Cary Grant.

Caryl variant form of **Carol.**

Carys (f) [kar-is]
From Welsh meaning 'love'.

Cass familiar form of **Cassandra**.

Cassandra (f)
From Greek, possibly a female form of **Alexander**. In Greek legend
Cassandra was a prophetess doomed not to be believed.
Familiar forms: **Cass, Cassie, Cassy**.

Cat familiar form of **Catherine**.

Cath familiar form of **Catherine**.

Catha familiar form of **Catherine**.

Cathal (m) [ka-hal]
From Irish Gaelic meaning 'battle' + 'strong'. It is sometimes
anglicized as **Charles**.
Familiar form: **Cal**.

Catharine variant form of **Catherine**.

Catherine (f)
Probably from Greek meaning 'pure'. One of the commonest female
names; the name of English Queens, of saints and of many famous
people. The 3rd-century St Catherine was tortured and put to death
on a spiked wheel for publicly confessing to being a Christian in
ancient Rome. There are many Catherines in literature and film,for
example, the heroine of *Wuthering Heights* by Emily Bronte.
Other forms: **Catharine, Cathryn,** Also many forms beginning with
'k' instead of 'c', because it was thought to be closer to the Greek
origin of the name: **Katharine, Katherin, Katherine, Kathryn,
Katarina**. Irish forms are: **Caitlìn, Cathleen** and **Kathleen**. The
Scottish Gaelic form is **Catriona** (anglicized as **Katrina**). The Welsh
form is **Catrin**.
Familiar forms: **Cat, Cath, Catha, Cathie, Cathy, Kath, Kathie,
Kathy, Kat, Kate, Kaety, Kay, Kit, Kittie, Kitty, Katie, Katy**.

Catrin Welsh form of **Catherine**.

Catriona (f) [ka-tree-na]
Scottish Gaelic form of **Catherine**, popular as a name in its own right,
especially in Scotland. It is the name of the heroine of Robert Louis
Stevenson's *Catriona* (1893).
Other form: **Katrina** (anglicized).

Ceallach see **Kelly**.

Cecelia variant form of **Cecilia**.

Cecil (m) [se-sil, see-sil, occasionally si–sil]
From Latin meaning 'blind' and the name of a family in ancient
Rome. Favoured at the end of the last century. Cecil Rhodes gave his
name to Rhodesia, now Zimbabwe.

Cecilia (f)
Female form of **Cecil**. St Cecilia was a 3rd-century pagan who
became a Christian, converted her husband and was put to death
with him. As she was a singer, she is the patron saint of music.
Variant forms: **Cecelia, Cecilie, Cicely**.

Cedric (m)
Possibly from Welsh **Cedrych**, or from a slip of the pen by Sir Walter
Scott, who, intending to call a character in *Ivanhoe* 'Cerdic', wrote
'Cedric' instead.

Cedrych (m)
From Welsh meaning 'welcome sight'.

Celeste (f)
From Latin meaning 'heavenly'.

Celia (f)
From **Caelius**, a Roman family name, separate in origin from **Cecilia**,
but frequently taken to be a short form of that name.
Other forms: **Sheila** from the Irish form **Síle**; see also **Sheila**.

Cesar variant form of **Caesar**.

Chad (m)
From Welsh meaning 'battle'. Chad was an Anglo-Saxon saint and bishop of Lichfield (d.672). Chad Varah is the founder of the Samaritans.

Chaim see Hyman.

Charity (f)
From the name of the virtue.
Familiar form: **Cherry.**

Charlene (f)
Female form of **Charles.**

Charles (m)
From the same Old English origin as **Carl**, meaning 'man'. The name has been consistently popular. Two English kings and the present Prince of Wales have borne the name. See also **Cathal.**
Familiar form: **Charlie.**

Charlotte (f)
Female form of **Charles.**
Familiar forms: **Charlie, Lottie, Lotty.**

Charmaine (f)
Sometimes thought of as a variant of **Charmian**, but more likely to be an invented name from a combination of 'charm' and the ending -*aine*.

Charmian (f)
From Greek meaning 'joy'. One of Cleopatra's ladies in waiting was Charmian, according to Shakespeare in *Antony and Cleopatra*.

Chelsea (f)
From the name of the London district. The daughter of Bill Clinton, President of the USA (1992-) has brought the name to prominence.

Chérie (f) [sheh-ree]
From French meaning 'darling'. It is the name of the wife of Tony Blair, elected leader of the British Labour party in 1994.

Other forms: **Cherry, Sheree, Sherry.**

Cherry (f)
The name of the fruit, but also often given as an English form of
Chérie and as a familiar form of **Charity**. In *Martin Chuzzlewit*,
Dickens created a character called Charity whose pet name was
Cherry.

Cheryl (f)
Invented in the early 20th century, perhaps by association with the
sound of names like **Shirley, Cherry** and **Beryl**.
Variant form: **Sheryl**.

Chester (m)
From the surname, itself from the place name of the capital city of
Cheshire, from Latin meaning 'camp'.
Familiar form: **Chet**.

Chloe (f) [klow-ee]
Biblical, perhaps from Greek meaning 'green'. In the New Testament
it is only mentioned briefly (1 Corinthians1:ll). Puritans used it
regularly in the 17th century.

Chris familiar form of **Christine, Christopher, Crystal**.

Chrissie familiar form of **Crystal, Christine**.

Christa familiar form of **Christabel, Christine**.

Christabel (f)
Perhaps from Latin meaning 'beautiful Christian'. Used by Coleridge
for the heroine of his poem *Christabel (1816)*.
Familiar form: **Christa**.

Christal variant form of **Crystal**.

Christel variant form of **Crystal**.

Christian (m)
From Latin meaning 'Christian'. It is the name of the hero of John Bunyan's *Pilgrim's Progress*.

Christiana variant form of **Christine**.

Christie familiar form of **Crystal, Christine, Christopher**.

Christina variant form of **Christine**.

Christine (f)
From Latin meaning 'Christian'.
Other forms: **Christiana, Christina**. Scottish forms: **Kirsten, Kirstin, Kirsteen** (last three Scottish).
Familiar forms: **Chris, Chrissie, Christie, Christa, Kirsty, Kirstie**.

Christopher (m)
From Greek meaning 'the bearer of Christ' from the legend of St Christopher who carried the infant Jesus to safety across a river. The saint is the patron of travellers.
Familiar forms: **Chris, Christie, Christy, Kit**.

Christy familiar form of **Crystal, Christopher**.

Chrystol variant form of **Crystal**.

Chrysty familiar form of **Crystal**

Ciara (f)
From Irish Gaelic meaning 'dark', it was the name of a 7th-century saint.
Variant form: **Kiera** (anglicized).

Ciarán see **Kiaran**.

Cicely variant form of **Cecilia**.

Cilla familiar form of **Priscilla**.

Cillian see **Killian**.

Cindy (f)
Familiar form of **Lucinda**, used as a name in its own right. Sometimes considered to be a familiar form of **Cinderella**, itself not normally used.
Variant form: **Sindy.**

Claire French form of **Clare.**

Clara [kler-ra or klah-ra] variant form of **Clare.**

Clare (f)
From Latin meaning 'clear'. St Clare was a 13th-century follower of St Francis. She founded the order of nuns called the Poor Clares.
Other forms: **Clara, Claire** (French).

Clarence (m)
From the title 'Duke of Clarence' usually conferred on younger sons or brothers of the English King.

Clarice (f)
From Latin meaning 'bringer of fame'.
Other form: **Clarissa.** This is the name of the heroine of Samuel Richardson's 18th-century novel about a girl who is a model of virtue.
Familiar form: **Clarrie.**

Clarissa variant form of **Clarice.**

Clarrie familiar form of **Clarice.**

Claud variant form of **Claude.**

Claude (m)
From the name of a family in ancient Rome meaning 'lame'. A famous member of the clan was the Emperor Claudius who initiated the Roman conquest of Britain in 43 AD.
Other form: **Claud.**

Claudette (f)
French female form of **Claude**.

Claudine French female form of **Claude**.

Clem familiar form of **Clement, Clementine**.

Clement (m)
From Latin meaning 'merciful'. Many popes took this name after an early saint who helped make Alexandria a centre of Christian learning. Clement Attlee was a Labour Prime Minister (1945-51). Familiar form: **Clem**.

Clementina variant form of **Clementine**.

Clementine (f)
Female form of **Clement**. The song of the 19th-century goldrush era in America *Oh my darling Clementine* popularized the name. The name of Winston Churchill's wife was Clementine.
Variant form: **Clementina**.
Familiar forms: **Clem, Clemmie**.

Cleo familiar form of **Cleopatra**.

Cleopatra (f)
From Greek meaning 'father's glory'. The Egyptian Queen famed for her beauty and love of Mark Antony has made this name eternal, but it is little used.
Familiar form: **Cleo**. This is much preferred and is a name in its own right. Cleo Lane is a famous singer.

Cliff familiar form of **Clifford**.

Clifford (m)
From the surname, itself a place name meaning 'ford at the cliff'. Familiar form: **Cliff**.

Clive (m)
From a place name in Cheshire and Shropshire meaning 'at the cliff'.

Clodagh (f)
From the name of an Irish river.

Clyde (m)
From the surname, itself from the Scottish river name. Clyde was the partner of Bonnie in a modern American gangster film.

Coinneach see **Kenneth.**

Colette (f)
A French form of **Nicola.** St Colette reformed the order of the Poor Clare nuns in the 15th century. Colette, the French novelist has made the name world famous this century.

Colin (m)
Although originally from **Nicholas,** it has long been used as a name in its own right. In Scotland it is taken to be an English form of Scottish Gaelic **Cailean** meaning 'youth'.
Other form: **Collin.**

Colleen (f)
From Irish meaning 'girl'. Little used in Ireland, but popular elsewhere.

Collin variant form of **Colin.**

Con familiar form of **Conor, Conrad, Constance, Constantine.**

Conan (m)
From Irish Gaelic meaning 'hound or wolf''. It is famous from Sir Arthur Conan Doyle (1859-1930), author of the Sherlock Holmes stories.

Conchobar see **Conor.**

Connie familiar form of **Constance.**

Conor (m)
From Irish Gaelic **Conchobar** possibly meaning 'lover of hounds'.

Conor Cruise O'Brien is a distinguished modern Irish historian and politician.
Variant form: **Connor**.
Familiar form: **Con**.

Conrad (m)
From Germanic meaning 'brave counsel'.
Variant form:**Konrad**.
Familiar form: **Con**.

Constance (f)
From Latin meaning 'firmness, constancy'.
Familiar forms: **Connie, Con**.

Constantine (m)
From Latin meaning 'firmness, constancy'. Little used after the 19th century. It was borne by the 4th-century Roman Emperor who made Christianity the official religion of the Empire.
Familiar form: **Con**.

Cora (f)
From Greek meaning 'maiden'. James Fennimore Cooper invented the name for the heroine of *The Last of the Mohicans* (1826).

Coral (f)
Like other names of jewels it came into use at the end of the 19th century.
Other form: **Còralie** .

Cordelia (f)
From the German martyr, St Cordula, whose name is probably from Latin meaning 'heart'. Cordelia was the youngest daughter in Shakespeare's *King Lear*.
Familiar form: **Delia**.

Corin variant form of **Corinne**.

Corinna variant form of **Corinne**.

Corinne (f)
French from a Greek name meaning 'maiden', popularized by
Madame de Stael's novel *Corinne* (1807).
Variant forms: **Corin,Corinna.**

Craig (m)
From the Scottish surname, itself from Scottish Gaelic meaning 'rock'.

Crispin (m)
From Latin meaning 'curly'. St Crispin was the patron saint of
shoemakers.

Cristal variant form of **Crystal.**

Crystal (f)
From the name of the cut glass, derived from Greek meaning 'ice'.
Variant forms: **Chrystal, Cristal, Crystle, Chrystol, Christal,
Christel, Krystal, Krystle.**
Familiar forms: **Chris, Chrissie, Christie, Christy, Chrystie.**

Cuthbert (m)
From Old English meaning 'famous' + 'bright'. St Cuthbert was a 7th-
century saint, missionary and prior of Lindisfarne monastery in
Northumberland.

Cynthia (f)
From Greek, a title of the goddess of the moon. The name was much
used in literature in past centuries.

Cyril (m)
From Greek meaning 'lord' or 'ruler'. The 9th-century Greek saint is
said to have invented the cyrillic alphabet used for the Russian
language.

Cyrus (m)
From Persian, possibly meaning 'shepherd'. Cyrus was the founder
of the Persian empire in 500 BC. Cyrus Vance was a well-known
American politician in the late 1970s.

Daffodil (f)
From the name of the flower. Occasionally used as a first name.
Familiar form: **Dilly.**

Dafydd Welsh form of **David.**

Dagmar (f)
Scandinavian, but sometimes used in Britain and the USA. Probably
from Old Norse, meaning 'day' + 'maid'.

Dai Welsh familiar form of **David.**

Dáibhí Irish Gaelic form of **David.**

Daibhidh Scottish Gaelic form of **David.**

Daisy (f)
From the name of the flower (based on Old English meaning 'day's
eye') in use from the end of the 19th century. Sometimes used as a
familiar form of Margaret as it resembles the French **Marguérite**
which means 'daisy'. It is the name of the heroine of Henry James's
novel *Daisy Miller* (1879).

Dale (m)
From the surname, itself based on the word meaning 'valley'.

Damhnait see **Dymphna.**

Damian (m)
From Greek meaning 'to tame'. St Damian, a 4th-century Greek
martyr, is the patron saint of doctors.
Variant forms: **Damien, Damon.** The musical *Guys and Dolls* was
based on gangster stories by the American writer Damon Runyon
(1884-1946). Damon Hill is a famous formula one motor racing
driver.

Dan (m)
Familiar form of **Daniel,** used as a name in its own right.

Daniel (m)
Biblical, from Hebrew, meaning 'God has judged'. The Book of
Daniel recounts the life of Daniel who was captured from Jerusalem
and taken into captivity in Babylon. For insisting on praying, he was
cast into the lions' den, but was miraculously saved. Common this
century also in literature from *The Book of Daniel* by L Doctorow to
Danny Champion of the World by Roald Dahl.
Familiar forms: **Dan, Dannie, Danny,** sometimes used as names in
their own right.

Daniella (f)
Female form of **Daniel**.
Variant form: **Danielle.**

Dannie familiar form of **Daniel.**

Danny familiar form of **Daniel.**

Dante (m)
From Latin meaning 'steadfast'. This Italian name is sometimes given
in honour of the medieval poet Dante Alighieri (1265-1321).

Daphne (f)
From Greek meaning 'laurel bush'. According to Greek mythology,
the god Apollo fell in love with Daphne. She ran away, calling on the
gods to save her and she was turned into a tree. Daphne du Maurier
(1907-1989) was famous as a romantic novel writer.

Darcy (m and f)
From the Irish surname, itself of Norman-French origin and derived
from a French place name, Arcy. Its relative popularity in Ireland
suggests it may also be from Irish, meaning 'dark man'.

Darel variant form of **Darrell.**

Darran variant form of **Darren.**

Darrell (m)
From the surname, of Norman-French origin, itself based on a place
name, Airelle, in France.

Variant forms: **Darel, Darrel, Darryl, Daryl.**

Darren (m)
Possibly from an Irish surname which began to be used as a first name this century.
Variant form: **Darran.**

Darryl variant form of **Darrell.**

Daryl variant form of **Darrell.**

Daunat variant form of **Dymphna.**

Dave familiar form of **David.**

David (m)
Biblical, from Hebrew, probably meaning 'beloved'. In the Old Testament (Samuel 1 and 2) the life of David, King of the Israelites, is recounted, including his victory over the giant Goliath. Two Scottish kings and several English princes have borne the name and the 6th-century St David is the patron saint of Wales.
Other forms: **Dafydd** (Welsh), **Dewi** (Welsh), **Daibhidh** (Scottish Gaelic [**dye**-vee]), **Dáibhí** (Irish Gaelic).
Familiar forms: **Dai** (Welsh), **Dave, Davie, Davy** (last two popular in Scotland). Playing on the frequency of the name, childrens' writer, Dr Seuss, wrote of Mrs McCave whose 24 sons were all called Dave.

Davina (f)
Scottish female form of **David.**

Davy familiar form of **David.**

Dawn (f)
Meaning 'the dawn'.

Deaglán see **Declan.**

Dean (m)
From the surname, itself from two sources, from Old English, meaning a 'valley', or from Latin, meaning an ecclesiastical dean.

Deanna (f)
Possibly a female form of **Dean**, or a re-make of **Edna**, made popular
by the 1940s film star Deanna Durbin. It can also be a variant form of
Diana.

Deb familiar form of **Deborah**.

Debbie familiar form of **Deborah**.

Deborah (f)
Biblical, from Hebrew, meaning 'bee'. In the Old Testament (Judges
4-5), Deborah, wife of Lapidoth, is judge and leader of the Israelites
against the Canaanites. She is also a poetess. There is also another
Deborah, the nurse of Rebecca, in Genesis 35:8.
Familiar forms: **Deb, Debbie, Debs.**
Variant form: **Debra.**

Debs familiar form of **Deborah**.

Declan (m)
From the Irish Gaelic name **Deaglán**, of uncertain origin. It was the
name of a 5th-century Irish bishop.

Dee (m and f)
Originally a familiar form of many names (such as Dennis or
Dorothy) beginning with the letter D, now used as a name in its own
right. For some bearers it is associated with the River Dee.

Deforest (m) [dee-for-est]
American name probably adopted in honour of John Deforest, the
American author. Deforest Kelly is an American actor famous for his
role as Dr 'Bones' McCoy in the TV series *Star Trek*.
Variant form: **Deforrest.**

Dek familiar form of **Derek**.

Deirdre (f)
Of uncertain origin, but famous as the name of the legendary Irish
princess, Deirdre of the Sorrows, who jilted her betrothed, the King

of Ulster, to elope with her lover to Scotland. The king murdered her lover and she died of a broken heart. Popurarized during the Celtic Revival in Ireland, particularly from Yeat's *Deirdre* (1907), and Synge's *Deirdre of the Sorrows* (1910).
Familiar form: **Didi.**

Del familiar form of **Delroy.**

Delia (f)
From the Greek, meaning 'of Delos', an island where the goddess Artemis was born; thus Delia is one of her titles. It is also a familiar form of **Cordelia, Adelia.**

Delila variant form of **Delilah.**

Delilah (f)
Biblical, from Hebrew; of uncertain meaning. The name of Samson's mistress. She tricked him into revealing that his strength lay in his hair, cut it off while he slept and betrayed him to his enemies.
Variant form: **Delila.**

Della (f)
Familiar form of **Adela**, used as a name in its own right.

Delphine (f)
From Latin **Delphina** meaning 'woman from Delphi'.

Delroy (m)
Probably an altered form of **Leroy**, from *le roy* meaning 'the king' in old French.
Familiar forms: **Del, Roy.** Delroy Wilson is a reggae artist of the 1990s.

Delwyn (f)
From Welsh, meaning 'beautiful, neat, white'.

Delyth (f)
From Welsh, meaning 'beautiful, neat'.
Denis variant form of **Dennis.**

Denise (f) [de-neez]
French female form of **Dennis**, now widely used in the English-
speaking world.
Familiar form: **Dennie** (also used as a name in its own right).

Dennie familiar form of **Denise, Dennis, Denton, Denzil.**

Dennis (m)
From **Denys,** derived from **Dionysius,** the Latin form of the name of
the Greek god of wine. Many saints, including the French patron St
Denys have borne the name as well as many writers and actors, such
as Dennis Potter and Dennis Price.
Other forms: **Denys, Denis.**
Familiar form: **Dennie, Denny, Dinny.**

Denny familiar form of **Dennis, Denton, Denzil.**

Denton (m)
From the surname, itself based on a place name meaning 'settlement
in a valley'.
Familiar forms: **Dennie, Denny.**

Denys variant form of **Dennis.**

Denzil (m)
From the surname, itself derived from Denzell, the name of a place in
Cornwall. Denzil is the hero of Arnold Bennett's *The Card* (1911).
Familiar forms: **Dennie, Denny.**

Derek (m)
A variant of **Theodoric** (meaning 'people's ruler') but long
established as a name in its own right.
Variant forms: **Derrick, Dirk.**
Familiar form: **Dek.**

Dermot (m)
From Irish Gaelic **Diarmaid,** perhaps meaning 'without envy'.
Other forms: **Diarmid, Kermit.**
Derrick variant form of **Derek.**

Dervla (f)
From Irish Gaelic meaning 'poet's daughter'. Dervla Murphy is a
20th-century travel writer and long-distance cyclist.

Désirée (f)
French, meaning 'desired'. Annemarie Selinko's novel *Desirée* (1953)
tells the story of a Frenchwoman Désirée Clary who became Queen of
Sweden.

Desmond (m)
From the Irish surname, itself from Irish Gaelic meaning 'South
Munster'.

Dewi Welsh form of **David**.

Di familiar form of **Diana**.

Diana (f)
Of uncertain origin. It is the Latin name of the goddess of the moon,
the pure and lovely huntress. When Prince Charles married Diana
Spencer in 1981, the name gained popularity.
Variant forms: **Deanna, Diane, Dianne, Dionne.** Dionne Warwick is
a famous singer.
Familiar form: **Di.**

Diane, Dianne variant forms of **Diana**.

Diarmaid see **Dermot**.

Diarmid variant form of **Dermot**.

Dick, Dickie, Dicky familiar forms of **Richard**.

Didi familiar form of **Deirdre**.

Dill familiar form of **Dylan**.

Dillan variant form of **Dylan**.

Dillon variant form of **Dylan**.

Dilly (f)
Originally a familiar form of **Daffodil** and **Dilys**, it is a name in its own right. Dilly Barlow has been well-known on radio since the 1980s.

Dilys (f)
From Welsh, meaning 'sincere'
Familiar form: **Dilly**.

Dina variant form of **Dinah**.

Dinah (f)
Biblical, from Hebrew meaning 'vindicated' or 'judged'. In the Old Testament (Genesis 34), Dinah, daughter of Jacob, was seduced by Shechem.
Variant form: **Dina**.

Dinny familiar form of **Dennis**.

Dionne variant form of **Diana**.

Dirk variant form of **Derek**.

Dod Scottish familiar form of **George**.

Dodie (f)
Familiar form of **Dorothy**. Dodie Smith was a 20th-century English writer, author of *101 Dalmations*..
Variant form: **Dody**.

Doirind see **Doreen**.

Dola familiar form of **Dolores**.

Dolina (f)
Female form of **Donald**, used in the Highlands of Scotland.

Doll familiar form of **Dorothy**, or in Scotland of **Dolina**.

Dolly familiar form of **Dolores, Dorothy** and in Scotland of **Dolina.**

Dolores (f)
From Spanish, meaning 'sorrows'. One of the titles given to the
Virgin Mary and therefore respected by Catholics.
Familiar forms: **Dola, Dolly, Lola, Lolita.**

Dolphus variant form of **Adolphus.**

Dom familiar form of **Dominic, Dominique.**

Dòmhnall see **Donald.**

Dominic (m)
From Latin, meaning 'lord'. St Dominic made this a respected name
from the 13th century onwards.
Familiar form: **Dom.**

Dominique French female form of **Dominic.**
Familiar form: **Dom.**

Don familiar form of **Donald.**

Dónal Gaelic form of **Donald.**

Donald (m)
From Scottish Gaelic, meaning 'world power'. It is the name of a clan.
Other forms: **Dòmhnall** (Scottish Gaelic), **Dónal** (Irish Gaelic).
Familiar forms: **Don, Donnie, Donny.**

Donalda female form of **Donald,** used in the Scottish Highlands.

Donna (f)
Italian, meaning 'lady'. A recent first name in English-speaking
countries.

Donncha, Donnchadh see **Duncan.**

Donnie familiar form of **Donald.**

Donny familiar form of **Donald.**

Donovan (m)
From the Irish Gaelic surname meaning 'dark'.

Dora (f)
Derived from **Dorothy** and **Theodora,** but long used as a name in its own right since Charles Dickens called the wife of David Copperfield Dora Spenlow.

Dorcas (f)
From Greek meaning 'gazelle'. It was used by the early Christians and later by the Puritans in the 17th century.

Doreen (f)
Derived from **Dora** but used as a name in its own right. (The addition of 'een' has transformed a number of names.) Also used as an anglicized form of Irish Gaelic **Doirind** (possibly meaning 'daughter of Finn').

Dorian (m)
From Greek, meaning 'man from Doris', a place in Greece. In *The Picture of Dorian Gray* (1891), Oscar Wilde portrayed a man whose portrait aged while he himself stayed young.

Doris (f)
Greek, meaning 'woman from Doris' a place in Greece. In Greek mythology, Doris was an immortal sea nymph. The film star Doris Day made the name famous in modern times.

Dorothea (f)
From Greek meaning 'gift of God'. Dorothea Casaubon is the heroine of George Eliot's *Middlemarch* (1872).
Other form: **Dorothy,** the most common English form.
Familiar forms: **Dodie, Dolly, Doll, Dot, Thea.**

Doug familiar form of **Dougal** or **Douglas.**

Dougal (m)
From Gaelic, meaning 'dark stranger'. It was originally used by the Irish to refer to the Danes in the 9th century.
Other forms: **Dugald, Dughall** (Scottish Gaelic) **Dubhghall** (Irish Gaelic).

Dougie familiar form of **Dougal** or **Douglas**.

Douglas (m)
From the Scottish surname, itself based on a place name, meaning 'dark stream'.
Familiar forms: **Doug, Dougie** [duggy or doogy].

Drena familiar form of **Adrienne**.

Drew familiar form of **Andrew**, used as a name in its own right.

Drina familiar form of **Adrienne**.

Drummond (m)
From the Scottish surname, itself based on a place name.

Drusilla (f)
From the Roman family name **Drausus**.

Duane (m)
From Irish Gaelic meaning 'dark'.
Variant forms: **Dwane, Dwayne**.

Dud familiar form of **Dudley**.

Dubhghall Irish Gaelic form of **Dougal**.

Dudley (m)
From the surname, itself based on a place name meaning ' Dudda's place or clearing'. Dudley Moore (1939-) is a noted musician and comedian.
Familiar form: **Dud**.

Duff (m)
From the surname, itself from Scottish Gaelic meaning 'black, dark'.

Dughall see **Dougal.**

Dugald variant form of **Dougal.**

Duke (m)
Possibly from the name **Marmaduke**, but used as a name in its own right, for example, by Duke Ellington, jazz musician (1899-1974).

Dulcie (f)
From Latin, meaning 'sweet'.

Duncan (m)
From Gaelic, meaning 'brown warrior'. It was the name of two early Scottish kings; Duncan I was murderd by Macbeth as narrated in Shakespeare's *Macbeth*.
Other forms: **Donncha** (Irish Gaelic), **Donnchadh** (Scottish Gaelic).

Dunstan (m)
From a place name, meaning 'stony hill'. St Dunstan was a 10th-century monk who was a hermit and later became abbot of Glastonbury.

Dustin (m)
From the surname, itself based on a place name, perhaps from Old Norse meaning 'Thor's stone'. Famous as the name of two actors, Dustin Farnum and Dustin Hoffman.
Familiar form: **Dusty.**

Dusty (m and f)
Originally a familiar form of **Dustin**, used as a name in its own right, both for males and females.

Dwane variant form of **Duane.**

Dwayne variant form of **Duane.**

Dwight (m)
From the surname which itself comes from the medieval female name **Diot**, no longer in use (from **Dionysos**). The American president Dwight D Eisenhower (1890-1969) made this a popular first name in the USA.

Dylan (m)
From Welsh, meaning possibly 'from the sea', after a sea god. Universally known because of the Welsh poet, Dylan Thomas (1914-1953) in whose honour Bob Dylan, pop singer, changed his original surname to Dylan.
Variant form: **Dillan, Dillon.**
Familiar form: **Dill.**

Dymphna (f) [dimf-na]
From the Irish Gaelic name **Damhnait** [dow-nit], meaning 'little fawn', the name of a 6th-century Irish saint.
Variant forms: **Dympna, Daunat.**

Dympna variant form of **Dymphna.**

Eachann see **Hector.**

Ealasaid Scottish Gaelic form of **Elizabeth.**

Éamon Irish Gaelic form of **Edmund.**

Éamonn Irish Gaelic form of **Edmund.**

Ean variant form of **Ian.**

Eanraig Scottish Gaelic form of **Henry.**

Earl (m)
From Old English meaning 'chieftain'.
Variant form: **Erle.**

Earlena variant form of **Earlene.**

Earlene (f)
Female form of **Earl** used mainly by black Americans.
Variant forms: **Earlena, Erleen, Erlean, Erlinda.**

Earnest variant form of **Ernest.**

Eartha (f)
From Old English meaning 'earth', not common but well known
because of the singer Eartha Kitt.

Ebanezer variant form of **Ebenezer.**

Eben familiar form of **Ebenezer.**

Ebeneezer variant form of **Ebenezer.**

Ebenezar variant form of **Ebenezer.**

Ebenezer (m)
Biblical, from Hebrew meaning 'stone of help' referring to the Old
Testament story of how Samuel set up a stone to commemorate the
Israelites' victory over the Philistines with the help of God (I Samuel
4). Like many Biblical names it was long popular, but its decline in
popularity was aided by the negative character of Ebenezer Scrooge
in Charles Dickens' *Christmas Carol.*
Variant forms: **Ebanezer, Ebeneezer, Ebenezar.**
Familiar form: **Eben.**

Ed familiar form of **Edgar, Edward, Edmund.**

Eda familiar form of **Edith, Edna.**

Eddie familiar form of **Edgar, Edward, Edmund.**

Eddy familiar form of **Edgar, Edward, Edmund.**

Eden (m and f)
From Hebrew meaning 'delight' and another name for 'paradise'.

Edgar (m)
From Old English meaning 'happiness' or 'prosperity' + 'spear'. It is
the name of Gloucester's virtuous son in *King Lear* and also of the
hero of *The Bride of Lammermuir* by Sir Walter Scott. It is one of many
names formed from Old English 'ead'- which means 'happiness' or
'prosperity'.
Familiar forms: **Ed, Eddie, Eddy.**

Edie familiar form of **Edith.**

Edith (f)
From Old English meaning 'happiness' or 'prosperity'+ 'war', that is
probably 'victory'. It was an aristocratic Anglo-Saxon name and early
saint's name. It was borne by the 20th-century actress Dame Edith
Evans.
Variant forms: **Editha, Edythe, Edyth, Edytha.**
Familiar forms: **Eda, Edie.**

Editha variant form of **Edith.**

Edmond variant form of **Edmund.**

Edmund (m)
From Old English meaning 'happiness' or 'prosperity' + 'protector'.
Famous bearers include Edmund Halley (1656-1742) who predicted
the return of the comet named after him, Edmund Keane the
Victorian actor and Edmund Hillary conqueror of Everest.
Other forms: **Edmond;** Irish Gaelic forms are **Éamon, Éamonn.**
Familiar forms: **Ed, Eddie, Eddy, Ned, Neddy, Neddie..**

Edna (f)
From Hebrew meaning 'pleasure, delight' as in the Garden of Eden.
Familiar form: **Eda.**

Edric (m)
From Old English meaning 'happiness' or 'prosperity' + 'powerful'.
Variant form: **Edrick.**

Edward (m)
From Old English meaning 'happiness' or 'prosperity' + 'protector'.

A royal and also a saintly name chiefly because of Edward the
Confessor, it has always been popular. Famous 20th-century bearers
are Edward Kennedy, Edward Heath, Prince Edward (1964-)
Other forms: **Eideard** (Scottish Gaelic [ay-jard]).
Familiar forms: **Ed, Eddie, Eddy, Ned, Neddy, Ted, Teddy.**

Edweena variant form of **Edwina**.

Edwene variant form of **Edwina**.

Edwin (m)
From Old English meaning 'happiness' or 'prosperity' + 'friend'.
Variant form: **Edwyn**.

Edwina (f)
Female form of **Edwin**. Edwina Currie is an outspoken 20th-century
Conservative politician.
Other forms: **Edwyna, Edweena, Edwene**.

Edwyn variant form of **Edwin**.

Edwyna variant form of **Edwina**.

Edyth variant form of **Edith**.

Edytha variant form of **Edith**.

Effie familiar form of **Euphemia**.

Egan (m)
From Irish Gaelic **Aeducán** meaning 'little fire'. It is mainly used in
Ireland.

Egbert (m)
From Old English meaning 'sword' + 'shining'.

Eibhilín see **Eileen**.

Eideard Scottish Gaelic form of **Edward**.

Eilean variant form of **Eileen**.

Eileen (f)
From Irish Gaelic **Eibhlín, Aibhilín**. Spread by Irish immigrants fleeing the potato famine in the second half of the19th century, it was extremely popular until the mid 20th century,
Other forms: **Aibhilín** (probably in origin a form of Evelyn), **Aileen** (widely used in Scotland), **Eibhilín** (probably originally a form of Helen), **Eilean, Eilleen, Ilean, Ileen, Ileene, Ilene**.
Familiar forms: **Eily, Eiley**.

Eilidh cottish Gaelic form of **Helen**.

Éilís Irish Gaelic form of **Elizabeth**.

Eilish anglicized form of **Éilís**.

Eilleen variant form of **Eileen**.

Eiluned variant form of **Eluned**.

Eily familiar form of **Eileen**.

Eira (f) [air-ah]
From Welsh meaning 'snow'.

Eirlys (f) [air-lis]
From Welsh meaning 'snowdrop'.

Eithne variant form of **Ethne**.

Elaina variant form of **Elaine**.

Elaine (f)
From an Old French form of **Helen**, it became popular this century.
Variant forms: **Ellaine, Elayne, Elaina**.

Elanora variant form of **Eleanor**.

Elayne variant form of **Elaine**.

Elden variant form of **Eldon.**

Eldon (m)
From a surname, itself from a place name meaning 'Ella's mound'.
Variant form: **Elden.**

Eldred (m)
From Old English meaning 'old counsel'. Common in Anglo-Saxon
times, it has rarely been used since.

Eleanor (f)
Derived from the Greek **Helen,** but it has been a name in its own
right since Henry II married Eleanor of Aquitaine in the 12th century.
Edward I's Queen Eleanor is commemorated by the crosses which
Edward set up from Herdelie to London at places where her funeral
procession rested. A modern Eleanor was the wife of Roosevelt,
President of the USA during World War 11.
Other forms: **Elanora, Elinor, Elinora, Elenora, Elenorah, Ellenora,
Lenora, Lenore, Leonora.**
Familiar forms: **Ella, Nora, Nellie, Nelly.**

Elena (f)
Spanish and Italian form of **Helen.**

Elenora variant form of **Eleanor.**

Elenorah variant form of **Eleanor.**

Elfie familiar form of **Elfrida.**

Elfreda variant form of **Elfrida.**

Elfrida (f)
From Old English meaning 'elf' + 'strength'.
Variant form: **Elfreda.**
Familiar forms: **Elfie, Frida, Freda.**

Eli (m)
Biblical, from Hebrew meaning 'high'. In the Old Testament, it was
the name of the teacher of Samuel (I Samuel 1-3).
Variant form: **Ely.**

Elias Greek form of **Elijah.**

Elijah (m)
Biblical, from Hebrew meaning 'the Lord is God'. In the Old
Testament it was the name of a prophet (I and II Kings). It is now
popular amongst black Americans.
Other forms: **Elias** (Greek form), **Ellis.**

Elinor, variant form of **Eleanor.**

Elinora variant form of **Eleanor.**

Elisa other form of **Elizabeth.**

Elisabeth variant form of **Elizabeth.**

Elita (f)
Derived from Latin *electa* through French *élite* meaning 'chosen'.

Eliza other form of **Elizabeth.**

Elizabeth (f)
Biblical, from Hebrew meaning 'God is perfection'. Biblical bearers of
the name were the wife of Aaron, the mother of John the Baptist;
saints were Elizabeth of Portugal and of Hungary. Royal Elizabeths
include Elizabeth I and Elizabeth II and Elizabeth the Queen Mother.
Famous modern Elizabeths include the actress Elizabeth Taylor.
Other forms: **Elspeth, Elspet** (Scottish), **Elisabeth,Eliza, Elisa, Elza,**
Ealasaid (Scottish Gaelic [yal-a-satch]), **Éilís** (Irish Gaelic [ay-lish])
Familiar forms: **Bette, Bettina, Betty, Bet, Beth, Betsy, Betsey, Bess,**
Bessie, Bessy, Elsa, Ilse, Libby, Liese, Lisette, Liza, Liz, Lizzie,
Lizzy.

Ella (f)
Probably a short form of several names containing *el, ella,* such as

Eleanor or **Elvira**, now used as a name in its own right It is also a familiar form of **Ellen**. Ella Fitzgerald is a famous 20th-century jazz singer.

Ellaine variant form of **Elaine**.

Ellen (f)
Originally a variant form of **Helen**, but now used as a name in its own right.
Familiar forms: **Ella, Nell, Nelly, Nellie.**

Ellenora variant form of **Eleanor**.

Ellie (f)
Originally a familiar form of several names containing *el, ella,* but now often used as a name in its own right.

Elliot (m)
From the surname, itself from the Old French form of **Elias**, which derives ultimately from **Elijah**.

Ellis (m)
From the surname, itself from **Elias**, the Greek form of the Hebrew name **Elijah**.

Elsa (f)
Originally a familiar form of **Elizabeth**, but often used as a name in its own right.

Elsey variant form of **Elsie**.

Elsie (f)
An independent name but originally from **Elspeth**, a variant form of **Elizabeth**. At the end of the 19th century it was extremely popular, now much less so.
Variant form: **Elsey.**

Elspeth Scottish form of **Elizabeth**.

Elton (m)
From the surname, itself from a place name meaning 'Ella's settlement'. Made famous by pop singer Elton John.

Eluned (f) [eh-lin-id]
From Welsh meaning 'idol'.
Variant form: **Eiluned**.
Other form: **Lynette** (anglicized).

Elvira (f)
From the name of the Spanish town Elvira. The name of characters in the operas *Don Giovanni, Ernani* and *I Puritani*.

Elvis (m)
From Irish Gaelic from the name of St. Ailbhe, patron saint of Munster who baptised St David in Wales. In English it was often rendered **Alvy** or **Alby**, but Irish immigrations to the USA resulted in the form **Elvis**. Modern pop singers, Elvis Presley and Elvis Costello have made the name world famous.

Elwin (m)
From Old English meaning 'old friend'.
Variant form: **Elwyn**.

Ely variant form of **Eli**.

Elza variant form of **Elizabeth**

Em familiar form of **Emma, Emily, Emmeline**.

Emaline variant form of **Emmeline**.

Emanuel variant form of **Emannuel**.

Emblyn variant form of **Emmeline**.

Emelen variant form of **Emmeline**.

Emeline variant form of **Emmeline**.

Emerson (m)
From the surname meaning 'son of **Emery**'.
Variant form: **Emmerson**.

Emery (m)
From the Germanic name **Amalric** meaning 'powerful noble'.
Variant form: **Emory** (especially in the USA).

Emil (m)
From the Roman family name **Aemilius**, meaning 'eager'.
Other form: **Émile** (French) made famous by the French writer Émile
Zola (1840-1902).

Emiley variant form of **Emily**.

Emilia see **Amelia**.

Emilie variant form of **Emily**.

Emiline variant form of **Emmeline**.

Emily (f)
From **Aemilia**, the feminine form of the Roman name **Aemilius**,
which means 'eager' and was the name of an important family in
ancient Rome. The Via Emilia is one of the great Roman roads in Italy
still in existence today.
Variant forms: **Emiley**, **Emilie**.
Familiar forms: **Em**, **Emmie**.

Emlyn (m and f)
The male name is after the Welsh town and is one of the names used
by the Welsh bards, winners of the national poetry competitons.
Common in Wales. As a female name, it is less common and has a
different origin, being derived from **Emmeline**.

Emma (f)
From Germanic meaning 'whole' or 'universal'. Popular throughout
the ages from the 11th century, when Ethelred's Queen bore it, to
today when it is often twinned with other names, as in: **Emma Jane**.

Famous bearers include Nelson's mistress, Lady Emma Hamilton
and the heroine of Jane Austen's novel *Emma* (1815).
Familiar forms: **Em, Emmie.**

Emmanuel (m)
Biblical, from Hebrew meaning 'God is with us'. The name in the
Bible given to the Messiah.
Variant form: **Emanuel, Immanuel.**
Familiar form: **Manny.**

Emmeline (f)
From Norman-French of Germanic origin, thought by some to mean
'work' or 'labour'.
Variant forms: **Emeline, Emiline, Emaline, Emblyn, Emelen,
Emylynn.** Note Welsh **Emlyn** has a different origin.
Familiar forms: **Em, Emmie.**

Emmerson variant form of **Emerson.**

Emmie familiar form of **Emma, Emily, Emmeline.**

Emory variant form of **Emery,** common in the USA.

Emrys (m)
Welsh form of **Ambrose,** itself from the Greek meaning 'immortal'.
Popular in Wales.

Emylynn variant form of **Emmeline.**

Ena (f)
Short form of **Helena,** now used as a name in its own right.

Enid (f)
From Welsh meaning 'soul' or 'life force'. It is the name of a character
in the medieval *Tales of King Arthur* and of the heroine in Tennyson's
Geraint and Enid, part of the *Idylls of the King* about King Arthur's
court. Enid Blyton was a famous children's writer of this century.

Enoch (m)
Biblical, from Hebrew meaning 'consecrated to God'. In the Old

Testament Enoch is the father of Methuselah (Genesis 5 18:24). Tennyson made it somewhat fashionable with *Enoch Arden,* a narrative poem about a seaman and his tragic love. Enoch Powell was a member of parliament famous for controversial views.

Ephraim (m)
Biblical, from Hebrew meaning 'fruitful'. In the Old Testament he was one of the sons of Joseph. The name is little used in modern times.

Eppie familiar form of **Euphemia.**

Erasmus (m)
From Greek meaning 'beloved'. Rarely used in modern times but borne by the famous 16th-century philosopher, Erasmus of Rotterdam, a leading scholar of the Renaissance. The writer Erasmus Darwin was the grandfather of Charles.

Eric (m)
From Old Norse meaning 'always' + 'ruler', made fashionable in the 19th century by the story of *Eric, or Little by Little,* by Frederic Farrar, also by stories of Eric the Red, discoverer of Greenland.
Variant forms: **Erick** and **Erik.**
Familiar forms: **Rick** and **Rickie.**

Erica (f)
The feminine form of **Eric,** but also often derived from the Latin for 'heather'.
Other form: **Erika.**
Familiar forms: **Rica, Rika.**

Erick, Erik variant forms of **Eric.**

Erika variant form of **Erica.**

Erin(f)
Perhaps from Irish Gaelic meaning 'western island' and popular as a female name in most places except Ireland.
Variant forms: **Errin** and **Eryn.**

Erle variant form of Earl.

Erlean variant form of Earlene.

Erleen variant form of Earlene.

Erlinda variant form of Earlene.

Erma see Irma.

Erna (f)
Female form of Ernest or Earnan (Irish for 'wise').
Ernest (m)
English form of Ernst meaning earnestness. It was extremely
fashionable at the end of the 19th century.
Variant form: Earnest.
Familiar form: Ernie.

Ernestina (f)
Female form of Ernest. It has declined in popularity in the 20th
century.
Variant form: Ernestine.

Ernie familiar form of Ernest.

Errin variant form of Erin.

Eryl (m and f)
From the Welsh meaning 'watcher' and said to be an name invented
by a Welsh family living in a house called Eryl y mor.

Eryn variant form of Erin.

Esau
Biblical, from a Hebrew word meaning 'rough and hairy'. This may
be because Esau in the Old Testament was born with his body
covered in hair (Genesis 25).

Esmaralda variant form of Esmeralda.

Esmé (f)
From French meaning 'respected' or 'esteemed'. Introduced into
Scotland by a visitor to the court of King James VI as a male name.
Now used only as a female name.

Esmeralda (f)
From the Spanish word for emerald, a green precious stone.
The name of the beautiful friend of the hunchback in Victor Hugo's
novel *The Hunchback of Notre Dame*. She wore a green jewel.
Variant form: **Esmaralda.**

Esmond (m)
From Old English meaning 'grace and protection'. Unaccountably
little used. It was a surname, as in *Henry Esmond* by Thackery and
had some popularity in the 19th century.

Esta familiar form of **Esther.**

Estella variant form of **Estelle.**

Estelle (f)
From Old French derived from Latin meaning 'star'. Charles Dickens
gave the name to the beautiful but heartless girl adopted by Miss
Havisham in *Great Expectations.*
Variant form: **Estella.**

Ester variant form of **Esther.**

Esther (f)
Biblical, from Persian meaning 'star' referring to the planet Venus.
The Biblical Esther saved the Jews in Persia from destruction by the
King's vizier. This is commemorated in the Jewish feast of Purim.
Variant forms: **Esta, Ester** and **Hester.**

Ethan (m)
From Hebrew meaning 'firmness and constancy'. More used in the
USA than in Britain.

Ethel (f)
From Old English meaning 'noble', an element in many names such as **Etheldreda**. Fashionable in the 19th century but little used now.

Ethelbert (m)
From Old English meaning 'noble' + 'bright'. The 6th-century King Ethelbert was converted by St Augustine. Little used now.

Etheldreda (f)
Latin version of an Old English word meaning 'noble strength'. The name of a 7th-century saint, Queen of Northumbria. Little used now. Other form: **Audrey** (which reflects the way the name came to be pronounced and is a much more usual form).

Ethne (f)
From Irish Gaelic probably meaning 'kernel'. The name was well known in Irish legend and early history, for example as the name of the mother of St Aidan.
Other forms: **Eithne, Ethnee, Ethnea, Aithne.**

Ethnea variant form of **Ethne**

Euan variant form of **Ewan.**

Eudora (f)
From Greek meaning 'good gift', a Greek sea goddess. One known bearer was the American writer Eudora Welty (1909-), but otherwise it is seldom used.

Eugene (m)
From Greek meaning 'well-born'; became a favourite in the English speaking world in the 19th century. The American playwright Eugene O'Neill (1888-1953) made it well-known.
Familiar form: **Gene** (widely used, especially in North America, as a name in its own right). Gene Hackman and Gene Wilder are American film stars.

Eugenie (f)
French female form of **Eugene**. An aristocratic name borne by the

wife of the Emperor Napoleon III, and more recently by the daughter of the Duke of York.

Eunice (f)
Biblical, from Greek meaning 'victorious'. In the New Testament Eunice was the mother of Timothy (II Timothy 1:5). Used seldom but consistently.
Variant form: **Unice.**

Euphemia (f)
From Greek meaning 'well regarded'. St Euphemia was a 4th-century martyr. In the Scottish Highlands it is used as an anglicized form of the Gaelic name **Oighrig** [oy-rik].
Familiar forms: **Effie, Eppie, Femie, Fanny.**

Eustace (m)
From Greek meaning 'fruitful'. The familiar forms have become more usual than the full form.
Familiar forms: **Stacey, Stacy.**

Eva familiar form of **Eve.**

Evan (m)
From Welsh **Ieuan**, itself a form of **John.**

Eve (f)
Biblical, from Hebrew meaning 'life'. In the Old Testament Eve is the wife of Adam (Genesis 2-4).
Familiar forms: **Eva, Evie.**

Eveline (f)
From the same origin as **Evelyn**. A popular name since Norman times. In the 18th century, Fanny Burney published a popular novel called *Evelina.*
Variant forms: **Evelina.** See also **Evelyn.**

Evelyn (m and f)
The original male name **Avelina** derived from the Germanic *Avila* or *Avilina*. Known today especially because of the writer Evelyn Waugh (1903-1966). See also **Eveline.**

Familiar form: **Evie.**

Evette variant form of **Yvette.**

Evie familiar form of **Eva, Evelyn.**

Evita (f)
Spanish diminutive of **Eva** which became a name in its own right, in vogue after a musical was made (1978) about the life of Evita Perón, wife of the ex-President of Argentina.

Evonne variant form of **Yvonne.**

Ewan (m)
From Scottish Gaelic **Eoghan,** probably meaning 'youth'. Since the 1960s, widespread outside Scotland.
Other forms: **Ewen, Euan.**

Ewart (m)
From the surname, itself derived from a place name meaning 'riverside settlement'. It was the middle name of the 19th-century Prime Minister, William Gladstone.

Ewen variant form of **Ewan.**

Ezekiel (m)
Biblical, from Hebrew meaning 'God give strength'; it was the name of a book of the Old Testament named after the prophet.

Ezra (m)
Biblical, from Hebrew meaning 'help'. The Book of Ezra forms part of the Old Testament. The name was used amongst early immigrants to America, but rarely now. A famous bearer was the American poet Ezra Pound (1885-1972).

Fabia (f)
Female form of the Roman family name **Fabius** (see **Fabian**).

Fabian (m)
From Latin **Fabianus**, from the Roman family name **Fabius**, possibly derived from Latin meaning 'bean'.

Fabiola (f)
From the same origin as **Fabia**; St Fabiola was a 4th-century saint. Queen Fabiola is the widow of the late King Baudouin, King of the Belgians.

Faith (f)
Now only a female name, it was used for both sexes by Puritans in the 17th century, referring to trust in God.
Familiar form: **Fay**.

Fanny familiar form of **Frances, Euphemia.**

Farquhar (m) [far-kher, far-ker]
From Scottish Gaelic **Fearchar**, meaning 'dear man' or 'friendly', it is used in the Highlands of Scotland.

Fay (f)
Familiar form of **Faith**. As a name in its own right, from an old word for 'fairy', used from the 19th century, when interest was high in the legends of King Arthur; his half-sister was the sorceress Morgan le Fay.
Variant form: **Faye**.

Fearghal see **Fergal.**

Fearghas see **Fergus.**

Felice (f)
Female form of **Felix**.

Felicia (f)
Female form of **Felix**.

Felicitas variant form of **Felicity**.

Felicity (f)
From Latin **Felicitas** (also occasionally used as a name), meaning 'happiness, good fortune', it was used by Puritans in the 17th century.
Familiar forms: **Flick, Liss, Lis, Lissa, Lissie, Phil.**

Felix (m)
From Latin meaning 'happy, fortunate', it was popular among early Christians and was the name of several saints.

Femie familiar form of **Euphemia.**

Fenella (f)
From Gaelic - see **Fionnuala.** It was the name of a character in Sir Walter Scott's *Peveril of the Peak.*
Variant forms: **Finella, Finola.**

Ferdi, Ferdie familiar forms of **Ferdinand.**

Ferdinand (m)
A Spanish name of Germanic origin, probably meaning 'journey' + 'ready', it was the name of several kings of Spain. (The modern Spanish form is **Hernán.**)
Familiar forms: **Ferdi, Ferdie.**

Fergal (m)
From Irish Gaelic **Fearghal**, meaning 'man' + 'valour'.

Fergie familiar form of **Fergus.** In the case of the Duchess of York, it is based on her maiden name, Ferguson.

Fergus (m)
From Gaelic **Fearghas**, meaning 'man' + 'bravery, strength', it is used in Scotland and Ireland.
Familiar form: **Fergie.**

Fern (f)
From the plant name, like so many others which have become popular this century.

Fi familiar form of **Fiona**.

Fifi (f)
French familiar form of **Josephine**, also used in the English-speaking world (but commoner as a name for a small dog!)

Finbar (m)
From Irish Gaelic **Fionnbharr** , meaning 'fair' + 'haired', it was the name of several early Irish saints. See also **Barry**.

Findlay variant form of **Finlay**.

Finella variant form of **Fenella**.

Finlay (m)
From Scottish Gaelic **Fionnlagh [fyoon-la]**, meaning 'fair' + 'warrior'. Other form: **Findlay** (though this is commoner as a surname).

Finn (m)
From Irish Gaelic **Fionn**, meaning 'fair'. It was the name of the legendary Irish hero, Finn MacCool (Fionn Mac Cumhaill).

Finola variant form of **Fenella**.

Fio familiar form of **Fiona**.

Fiona (f)
Possibly from Scottish Gaelic *fionn*, meaning 'fair'. It has been popular, especially in Scotland, since the 19th century when the Romantic poet William Sharpe wrote under the pen-name of Fiona Macleod.
Familar forms: **Fi, Fio**.

Fionnlagh see **Finlay**.

Fionnuala (f)
From Irish Gaelic **Fionnghuala** meaning 'fair-shouldered' (as Scottish form **Fionnghal** - see **Flora**).
Familiar form: **Nuala** (also used as a name in its own right).

Flavia (f)
Female form of Latin **Flavius**, from *flavus* meaning 'yellow(-haired)'.

Fleur (f) [floer]
From French meaning 'flower'. It gained popularity in the early 20th century from the name of the character Fleur Forsyte in *The Forsyte Saga* by John Galsworthy. The English form **Flower** is also occasionally used as a name.

Flick familiar form of **Felicity**.

Flo familiar form of **Flora**, **Florence**.

Flora (f)
From the Latin word for flower. Flora was the Roman goddess of flowers and of the spring, but the name became popular, especially in Scotland, in the 18th century, after Flora MacDonald, a Highland lady from the Isle of Skye who helped Prince Charles Edward Stuart ('Bonnie Prince Charlie') to escape to safety in France after the Battle of Culloden in 1746. In fact the name was used in the Scottish Highlands as an English form of the Gaelic **Fionnghal** [fyoon-a-ghal] meaning 'fair-shouldered'. See also **Fionnuala**.
Familiar form: **Flo**.

Florence (f)
From Latin **Florentius**, **Florentia**, from *florens* meaning 'flowering'. The name was formerly male as well as female. It was made popular as a female name in the 19th century by Florence Nightingale, the nursing reformer (who was, however, so named because she was born in the Italian town of Florence (Firenze)).
Familiar forms: **Flo**, **Florrie**, **Flossie**.

Flower see **Fleur**.

Floyd variant form of **Lloyd**.

Fra familiar form of **Francis**.

Fran familiar form of **Frances**.

Frances (f)
Female form of **Francis**. (It was formerly used also as a male name).
Familiar forms: **Fanny, Fran, Francie, Frankie**, occasionally **Frank**.

Francesca (f) [francheska]
Italian equivalent of **Frances**, feminine form of **Francesco**.

Francesco see **Francis**.

Francie familiar form of **Frances**, occasionally of **Francis**.

Francine (f) [fronseen]
Familiar form of **Francoise** (French form of **Frances**), used
occasionally in Britain.

Francis (m)
Used as an English (and French) form of Italian **Francesco**, meaning
French. It was widely used from the 16th century on, owing to the
popularity of Italian Renaissance culture. A strong influence was the
12th-13th-century St Francis of Assisi (whose nickname it was; his
baptismal name was Giovanni).
Familiar forms: **Fra, Frank** (also a name in its own right), **Frankie,
Francie, Franco**.

Frank (m, occasionally f)
From the name of the Germanic tribe who gave their name to France.
Used as a name in its own right and also as a familiar form of
Francis, Franklin, or occasionally of **Frances**.
Familiar form: **Frankie**.

Frankie familiar form of **Francis, Frank, Franklin**, and **Frances**.

Franklin (m)
From the surname, itself from Middle English meaning 'freeman'.
Made popular in the USA , after the 18th-century statesman
Benjamin Franklin and the 20th-century President Franklin D
Roosevelt.
Familiar forms: **Frank, Frankie**.

Fraser (m)
From the Scottish surname, itself Norman-French of uncertain origin,
now popular in Scotland as a first name.

Fred familiar form of **Frederick, Frederica,** and (less commonly) of
Alfred.

Freda (f)
Familiar form of **Winifred, Elfrida,** and occasionally of **Frederica;**
also used as a name in its own right.

Freddie, Freddy familiar forms of **Frederick,** and occasionally of
Frederica.

Frederica (f)
Female form of **Frederick**
Familiar forms: **Fred, Freddie, Freddy, Rica, Rika, Freda.**

Frederick (f)
Of Germanic origin, meaning 'peace' + 'ruler', it has been popular in
Britain, along with other German names since the Hanoverian kings
came to the throne in the 18th century.
Familiar forms: **Fred, Freddie, Freddy.**

Freya (f) [fraya]
The name of the Old Norse goddess of love, it is popular in Shetland
and Orkney. Freya Stark was an English travel writer and explorer of
the Middle East.

Frida familiar form of **Elfrida.**

Fulvia (f)
From the Roman family name **Fulvius,** from Latin meaning 'tawny,
yellowish-brown'.

Gab familiar form of **Gabriel.**

Gabbie familiar form of **Gabrielle.**

Gabriel (m) [gaybriel]
From Hebrew meaning 'man of God', it was the name of the
archangel who announced the forthcoming birth of Jesus to Mary (St
Luke 2:1). See also **Gay**.
Familiar forms: **Gab, Gay**.

Gabrielle (f) [gabriel]
French female form of **Gabriel**, also used in the English-speaking
world.
Familiar forms: **Gaby, Gabbie, Gay, Gaye**.

Gail (f)
Familiar form of **Abigail**, now used as a name in its own right.
Variant form: **Gale**.

Gardenia (f)
From the name of the flowering plant, itself called after Dr Alexander
Garden, an 18th-century Scottish naturalist.

Gareth (m)
From Welsh, probably meaning 'gentle', it was the name of a
character in the 16th-century *Morte d'Arthur* by Thomas Malory. Now
popular throughout Britain.
Variant form: **Garth**.
Familiar form: **Gar(r)y** (also a name in its own right).

Garfield (m)
From the surname, itself from a place name probably deriving from
Old English meaning 'triangle' + 'field'. It was the surname of a 19th-
century president of the USA and is popular in black American
families. It is also the name of a well-known cartoon cat!

Garry variant form of **Gary**.

Garth variant form of **Gareth**.

Gary (m)
Used as a familiar form of **Gareth**, but as a name in its own right it
comes from the surname. It has become popular in the 20th century,

especially after the film star Gary Cooper (who took this stage name from the town of Gary, Indiana).
Variant form: **Garry**.

Gaspard see **Jasper**.

Gavin (m)
Of Celtic origin, possibly meaning 'hawk'. In the form **Gawain**, it occurs in the legends of King Arthur as the name of one of the Knights of the Round Table. Used until the 16th century, but only in Scotland thereafter, until very recently when it became popular throughout the English-speaking world.

Gay (m and f)
As a female name it is simply the adjective meaning 'cheerful, happy'. It was popular in the earlier part of the 20th century, but is less so now because the word is used to mean homosexual. It is also used as a familiar form of **Gabrielle**.
As a male name, it is a familiar form of **Gabriel**.
Variant form: **Gaye**.

Gaylord (m)
From the surname, itself deriving from French *gaillard*, meaning 'a cheerful, lively person'.

Gaynor (f)
Medieval English form of **Guinevere**, popular in recent decades.

Gearóid Irish Gaelic form of **Gerald**.

Ged familiar form of **Gerard** or **Gerald**.

Gem familiar form of **Gemma**.

Gemma (f) [jemma]
From medieval Italian meaning 'gem, jewel'.
Variant form: **Jemma**.
Familiar form: **Gem**.

Gene (m) [jeen]
Familiar form of **Eugene**, now also used as a name in its own right.

Geneva (f)
Of doubtful origin. May be from the Swiss place name, or a variant of **Genevieve**, or perhaps of **Jennifer**.

Genevieve (f) [jeneveev]
From French, of uncertain origin. The 5th-century St Geneviève, the patron saint of Paris, was a nun who helped to save the people of Paris in attacks from the Huns and others. A popular name in France, it has been used in Britain since the 19th century.

Geoff familiar form of **Geoffrey**.

Geoffrey (m)
Norman-French of Germanic origin, it may be related to **Godfrey**, but its precise origin is unclear. Popular in the Middle Ages, as in the name of the 14th-century writer Geoffrey Chaucer, and again from the 19th century onwards. See also **Jepson**.
Variant form: **Jeffrey**.
Familiar forms: **Geoff, Jeff**.

Geordie familiar form of **George**.

George (m)
From Old French, through Latin from Greek meaning 'farmer'. Although St George was regarded as patron saint of England from the Middle Ages, the name only became popular there from the 18th century, when the Hanoverian kings brought a succession named George. It is also used as a familiar form of **Georgina** and of other female forms of the name.
Other forms: **Seòras, Deòrsa** (both Scottish Gaelic [shawras, dyawrsa], **Seoirse** (Irish Gaelic [shore-sa], **Sior, Sior(y)s** (both Welsh).
Familiar forms: **Georgie, Geordie** (especially in Scotland and in the North of England where it is used as a nickname for a person from the Newcastle area), **Dod** (Scottish).

Georgette, Georgia, Georgiana, Georgina (f)
Female forms of **George**, of which the last is the most popular.
Familiar forms: **Georgie, Gina, George.**

Georgie familiar form of **George** or of **Georgia, Georgina**.

Georgina see **Georgette**.

Ger familiar form of **Gerald, Gerard**.

Geraint (m) [ger-a-eent]
Welsh, possibly derived from Greek meaning 'old man', it is found in
several Welsh legends. Popular, especially in Wales, in the latter part
of the 20th century. Known more widely as the name of the opera
singer Geraint Evans.

Gerald (m) [jerald]
Norman-French of Germanic origin, meaning 'spear' + 'rule', it is
sometimes confused with **Gerard**. It was popular in the Middle Ages
and then again from the 19th century onwards; it remained popular
in Ireland throughout this time.
Other forms: **Gearóid** (Irish Gaelic [gyar-oaj], **Gerallt** (Welsh).
Familiar forms: **Gerry, Jerry, Ger, Ged, Jed.**

Geraldine (f) [jeraldeen]
Female form of **Gerald**.
Familiar form: **Gerry.**

Gerallt Welsh form of **Gerald**.

Gerard (m) [jerard]
Norman-French of Germanic origin, meaning 'spear' + 'strong,
brave', it is sometimes confused with **Gerald**.
Other forms: **Gerrard, Jerrard.**
Familiar forms: **Gerry, Jerry, Ger, Jed, Ged.**

Gerda (f) [gerda]
Scandinavian name which has been popular in these countries since
the 19th century. Also used occasionally in Britain.

Germaine (f) [jermain]
Female form of the French name **Germain**, from Latin *germanus* meaning 'brother'. Name of the Australian feminist writer Germaine Greer.

Gerry familiar form of **Gerald, Gerard,** or **Geraldine.**

Gert familiar form of **Gertrude.**

Gertie familiar form of **Gertrude.**

Gertrude (f) [gertrood]
Of Germanic origin, meaning 'spear' + 'strength', it was popular in the 19th century.
Familiar forms: **Gertie, Gert, Trudi** (from German), **Trudie, Trudy.**

Gervaise variant form of **Gervase.**

Gervase (m) [jervis]
Norman-French of doubtful origin, possibly connected with Germanic meaning 'spear'. St Gervasius was an obscure early saint. See also **Jarvis.**
Variant form: **Gervaise.**

Gib familiar form of **Gilbert**

Gibbie familiar form of **Gilbert.**

Gid familiar form of **Gideon.**

Gideon (m) [gid-ee-on]
Biblical from Hebrew, of uncertain meaning, it was the name of the Israelite leader who rescued them from the Midianites (Judges 6:14). It was popular with Puritans in the 17th century.
Familiar form: **Gid.**

Gil familiar form of **Gilbert.**

Gilbert (m)
Norman-French of Germanic origin, meaning 'pledge'+ 'bright', it

was popular in the Middle Ages and also in later centuries in Scotland and the North of England. It was used in the Highlands of Scotland as an English form of **Gille Brighde** (servant of St Bridget). Familiar forms: **Gib**, **Gibbie** (especially in Scotland), **Gil, Bert, Bertie**.

Gilberta (f)
Female form of **Gilbert**.

Giles (m)
Altered from Latin **Aegidius**, from Greek meaning 'kid, young goat'. St Giles was, according to tradition, an 6th-century Athenian saint who moved to France; he was the patron saint of cripples and blacksmiths. Many medieval churches were dedicated to him, including the High Kirk of Edinburgh.

Gill familiar form of **Gillian**.

Gilleasbaig see **Gillespie**.

Gillespie (m)
From the Scottish surname, itself from Scottish Gaelic **Gilleasbaig**, meaning 'servant of the bishop'. See also **Archibald**.

Gillian (f) [jilian]
Variant form of **Julian** (formerly occasionally used as a female name) or of **Juliana**. It was popular in the Middle Ages and again in the 20th century.
Variant form: **Jillian**.
Familiar forms: **Gill, Jill, Gilly, Gillie, Jilly, Jillie**.

Gina (f) [jeena]
Familiar form of **Georgina**, **Regina**, but also used as a name in its own right, probably often after the Italian film star Gina Lollobrigida.

Ginger (f)
As well as being a nickname for someone with red hair, it was popular for a time, after the Hollywood film star Ginger Rogers; in her case it was a familiar form of **Virginia**.

Ginny, Ginnie familiar forms of **Virginia**.

Giorsal Scottish Gaelic form of **Grace**.

Glad familiar form of **Gladys**.

Gladys (f)
From the Welsh **Gwladys**, regarded as a Welsh form of **Claudia**, it became popular in the late 19th century, but is now quite rare. Familiar form: **Glad**.

Glanville (m)
Form the surname, itself either from a Norman-French place name, or from Old English meaning 'clean' + 'field'.

Glen (m)
Probably from the Scottish surname, also common as a place name element, from Scottish Gaelic *gleann* a (narrow) valley. Popular as a first name, especially in Scotland, in the 20th century. It is also used as a familiar form of **Glenys**.
Variant form: **Glenn**.

Glenda (f)
From Welsh meaning 'clean, pure' + 'good'. It has become more widely known through the actress and MP Glenda Jackson.

Glendower anglicized form of **Glyndwr**.

Glenis variant form of **Glenys**.

Glenn variant form of **Glen**.

Glenna (f)
Female form of **Glen**.

Glenys (f)
From Welsh meaning 'pure, holy'. Well-known as the name of Glenys Kinnock, wife of the former Labour leader. ·
Variant forms: **Glenis, Glynis**.

Familiar forms: **Glen, Glyn**.

Gloria (f)
Latin meaning 'glory, fame'. First used as first name by George
Bernard Shaw in his play *You Never Can Tell* (1898), it was popular in
the first half of the 20th century.

Glyn (f)
Welsh meaning 'valley', used since the beginning of the century. It is
also used as a familiar form of **Glynis**; see **Glenys**.
Variant form: **Glynn**

Glyndwr (m) [glen-dow-er]
From Welsh meaning 'valley' + 'water'. It was adopted in the 20th
century by Welsh patriots in honour of Owain Glyndwr (1359-1416)
who conducted a guerilla war against King Henry V.
Other form: **Glendower** (anglicized). The Sons of Glendower are a
20th-century Nationalist group in Wales.

Glynis variant form of **Glenys**.

Glynn variant form of **Glyn**.

Godfrey (m)
Norman-French of Germanic origin, meaning 'God' + 'peace'. It has
often been confused with **Geoffrey**.
Other forms: **Goraidh** (Scottish Gaelic).

Godwin (m)
From Old English meaning 'God' + 'friend', now mainly a surname.

Golda see **Goldie**.

Goldie (f)
Referring to golden hair, known from the name of the American
actress Goldie Hawn. The Yiddish form **Golda** was brought to
prominence in the 1960s and 70s by the Israeli Prime Minister Golda
Meir.

Goraidh Scottish Gaelic form of **Godfrey**.

Gordon (m)
Scottish surname, deriving from a place name, possibly of ancient
Celtic origin meaning 'spacious' + 'fort'. It is now popular as a first
name, coming into wide use after the death of General Gordon at
Khartoum in 1885.

Grace (f)
From Latin *gratia*, referring to the religious quality. It became
popular among Puritans in the 17th century, and remained so in
Scotland and the North of England. Grace Darling was the daughter
of a lighthouse keeper whose bravery rescued sailors in a storm off
the Northumberland coast in 1838. In the 20th century its popularity
was increased by the actress Grace Kelly (1928-82) who became
Princess Grace of Monaco. See also **Gráinne**.
Other form: **Giorsal** (Scottish Gaelic [girsal])
Familiar form: **Gracie** (used as a stage name by the singer Gracie
Fields (1898-1979)).

Grady (m)
From the Irish surname, itself from Irish Gaelic meaning 'noble'.

Graeme variant form of **Graham**.

Graham (m)
Though derived from an English place name (Grantham in
Lincolnshire) of uncertain origin, it has been a prominent Scottish
surname since the Middle Ages. It is now also much used as a first
name outside Scotland, as in the name of the novelist Graham Greene
and the racing driver Graham Hill.
Other forms: **Graeme** (mainly used in Scotland), **Grahame** (less
common).

Gráinne(f) [grawnye]
Irish Gaelic, possibly meaning 'she who inspires terror' or 'grain
goddess', it was the name of the heroine of a well-known Irish
legend.
Other forms: **Grania, Granya** (anglicized); sometimes anglicized as
Grace.

Grant (m)
From the Scottish surname, of Norman-French origin, probably meaning 'big, tall'. Its popularity in the USA may have been due to the 19th-century president, Ulysses S Grant.

Granville (m)
From the surname, itself of Norman-French origin meaning 'large' + 'town'.

Granya variant form of **Gráinne**.

Greg familiar form of **Gregor** or **Gregory**.

Gregg familiar form of **Gregor** or **Gregory**.

Gregor (m)
Mainly Scottish form of **Gregory**. The Gaelic form **Griogair** gave rise to the clan name MacGregor, among whose many turbulent members was the 18th-century Rob Roy MacGregor, immortalized in Sir Walter Scott's novel.
Familiar forms: **Greg, Gregg, Greig** (the last from the surname).

Gregory (m)
From Greek meaning 'watchful', it was the name of several early saints and popes. It therefore lost favour in England after the Reformation but revived somewhat in the 19th century. It gained some popularity in the 1940s after the Hollywood star Gregory Peck.
Other form: **Grigor** (Welsh).
Familiar forms: **Greg, Gregg**.

Greig familiar form of **Gregor**.

Gresham (m)
From the surname, itself from an Old English place name meaning 'grazing' + 'hamlet'.

Greta (f) [greeta, gretta]
Familiar form of **Margaret**, common Swedish and German form, also used in Ireland and Scotland. It gained popularity in the mid 20th century after the Swedish film actress Greta Garbo.

Griff familiar form of **Griffith.**

Griffith (m)
From Welsh **Gruffydd,** of uncertain origin.
Familiar form: **Griff;** Griff Rhys Jones is a well-known comedian.

Grigor Welsh form of **Gregory.**

Griogair Scottish Gaelic form of **Gregor.**

Griselda (f) [grizelda]
Possibly of Germanic origin, meaning 'grey' + 'battle'. It was made
popular in the Middle Ages by the story of a long-suffering wife told
by Boccaccio, retold by Chaucer.
Variant form: **Grizel** (Scottish).
Familiar forms: **Zelda** (also used as a name in its own right), **Grizzie.**

Gruffydd see **Griffith.**

Gus familiar form of **Angus, Augustus, Gustave,** or of **Augusta.**

Gussie familiar form of **Augusta** or of **Gustave, Augustus.**

Gustave (m)
French form of the Scandinavian **Gustav,** meaning 'staff of Gautr', it
was the name of several Swedish kings. The French form has been
used occasionally in England.
Familiar forms: **Gus, Gussie.**

Guy (m)
Norman French name of Germanic origin, it lost popularity after the
Guy Fawkes plot in London in 1605, but revived again from the 19th
century.
Variant form: **Gye.**

Gwen (f)
Familiar form of **Gwendolyn,** now more popular than the original
name.

Gwendolen, Gwendoline variant forms of **Gwendolyn.**

Gwendolyn (f)
From Welsh meaning 'fair' + 'ring, circle', it is found in various forms
in Welsh legends. It became popular in the late 19th century.
Variant forms: **Gwendoline, Gwendolen, Wendoline.**
Familiar forms: **Gwen** (now commonly used as a name in its own
right), **Gwenda.**

Gwilim, Gwilym, Gwyllim Welsh form of **William.**

Gwladys see **Gladys.**

Gwyn (m)
Welsh meaning 'fair, blessed'.
Variant forms: **Gwynn, Wyn;** see also **Wynne.**

Gwyneth (f)
From Welsh meaning 'happiness', or altered from the place name
Gwynedd. Very popular in Wales, but also used elsewhere.

Gwynn variant form of **Gwyn.**

Gwynfor (m) [gwin-for]
From Welsh meaning 'blessed' or 'great' or 'white', the name was
coined in the 20th century.

Gye variant form of **Guy.**

Hadyn (m)
Of uncertain origin, but regarded as Welsh because of its spelling and
its popularity in Wales. It has been connected with the English
surname **Haddon,** meaning 'hill with heather', and also with the
Austrian composer Josef Haydn (1732-1809), whose music has been
much admired in Wales. Many Welsh people regard it as a Welsh
form of **Aidan.**
Variant forms: **Hayden, Haydon.**

Hagar (f)
Biblical, from Hebrew meaning 'forsaken'. In the Old Testament

(Genesis 16) Hagar, an Egyptian, was the maid of Sarah who bore a
son to Abraham. Hagar the Horrible is a well-known cartoon
character.

Hailey variant form of **Hayley**.

Hal (m)
Familiar form of **Henry**. The future King Henry V was known as
Prince Hal in Shakespeare's *King Henry IV*.

Haley variant form of **Hayley**.

Hallam (m)
From the surname, itself from place names derived from Old English
meaning either 'nook, corner' or 'rock, stone'

Hamish see **James**.

Hank familiar form of **Henry**, common in the USA.

Hannah (f)
Biblical, from Hebrew meaning '(God) has favoured me', it was the
name of the mother of Samuel in the Old Testament (1 Samuel 1:2),
and has always been a popular Jewish name. It was much used by
Protestants in Britain from the time of the Reformation and, though it
had lost ground by the early 20th century, it has recently regained
popularity. See also **Ann**. **Hannah** is sometimes used as a familiar
form of **Johannah**.

Harald Scandinavian form of **Harold**.

Harold (m)
From Old English meaning 'army' + 'ruler', influenced in the early
Middle Ages by the Old Norse **Haraldr**, with the same meaning.
Though popular at that time, it lost ground until the 19th century. It
was the name of two 20th-century British prime ministers, Harold
MacMillan and Harold Wilson.
Other forms: **Harald** (Scandinavian), **Arailt** (Scottish Gaelic [araltch]
Familiar form: **Harry**.

Harriet (f)
Female form of **Harry, Henry**, it is derived from French **Henriette**
and is sometimes used as a familiar form of **Henrietta**.
Familiar forms: **Hattie**, less commonly **Hettie**.

Harry (m)
Familiar form of **Henry, Harold**, the original form of the name in
English and still sometimes used as a name in its own right.

Hartley (m)
From the surname, itself from various place names, most of them
deriving from Old English meaning 'hart' + 'wood, clearing'.

Harvey (m)
From the surname, itself from a Breton name of Celtic origin,
probably meaning 'battle' + 'worthy'. Harvey Keitel is a well-known
actor.

Hattie familiar form of **Harriet**.

Hayden variant form of **Hadyn**.

Haydon variant form of **Hadyn**.

Hayley (f)
From the surname, itself from a place name, probably from Old
English meaning 'hay' + 'clearing'. Its use as a female name probably
began with the actress Hayley Mills, daughter of John Mills; it was
her mother's middle name.
Variant forms: **Hailey, Haley**.

Hazel (f)
From the tree name, popular in Britain since the late 19th century.

Headley variant form of **Hedley**.

Heath (m)
From the surname, itself from the word meaning 'an area with wild
plants'.

Heather (f)
From the plant name, used since the late 19th century, and popular
especially in Scotland, where the plant grows abundantly.

Hebe (f) [hee-bi]
From Greek meaning 'young'. Hebe was the Greek goddess of
youth, daughter of Zeus, and cupbearer to the gods. The name was
popular for a time in the late 19th century.

Heck familiar form of **Hector**.

Heckie familiar form of **Hector**.

Hector (m)
From Greek, probably meaning 'holding fast', it was the name of
Trojan hero, son of King Priam, who was killed by Achilles. Popular
in the Highlands of Scotland where it is used as a substitute for the
Gaelic name **Eachann** (though there doesn't seem to be any
connection between the names).
Familiar forms: **Heck, Heckie** (Scottish).

Hedley (m)
From the surname, itself from several place names in the north of
England, deriving from Old English meaning 'heather' + 'clearing'.
Variant forms: **Headley, Hedly**.

Heidi (f) [high-dee]
Swiss-German familiar form of **Adelheid**, German form of **Adelaide**.
Its use in Britain is probably due to the children's story *Heidi* (1881)
by Johanna Spyri.

Helen (f)
From Greek, possibly meaning 'bright, shining', it was the name of
the Trojan 'heroine' whose beauty caused the Trojan War. It was
made popular in Europe by the 3rd-century Saint Helena, mother of
the Emperor Constantine. She was said to have been born in Britain,
which added to the popularity of the name there in the Middle Ages.
In the past the form **Ellen** was more popular in England and the USA
but Helen has always been widely used in Scotland. See also **Elaine,
Eleanor**.

Other forms: **Ellen, Helena, Eilidh** (Scottish Gaelic [ay-lee],
anglicized as **Ailie**), **Léan** (Irish Gaelic), **Elena** (Spanish and Italian),
Ilona (Hungarian).
Familiar forms: **Nell, Nellie, Nelly, Lena, Ena.**

Helena variant form of **Helen.**

Helga (f)
German and Scandinavian name, derived from Old Norse, meaning
'prosperous', it is also used in the English-speaking world.
Other form: **Olga** (Russian).

Henrietta (f)
Female form of **Henry.** It was first used in Britain in the 17th century
after Queen Henrietta Maria, wife of Charles I. It is sometimes used
in the Highlands of Scotland as a substitute for the Gaelic name
Oighrig.
Familiar forms: **Harriet** (also used as a name in its own right), **Hetty,
Hatty, Etta, Netta, Henny.**

Henry (m)
Norman French of Germanic origin, meaning 'home ruler', it was the
name of eight kings of England between the 11th and the 16th
centuries. The usual form in England until the 17th century was
Harry.
Other forms: **Eanraig** (Scottish Gaelic [ayn-rik], **Anraoi** (Irish Gaelic).
Familiar forms: **Harry, Hal, Hank** (popular in the USA).

Herb familiar form of **Herbert.**

Herbert (m)
Norman-French of Germanic origin, meaning 'army' + 'bright', it was
popular in the early Middle Ages and again in the 19th century.
Familiar forms: **Herb, Herbie, Bert, Bertie.**

Hercules (m)
From Latin, deriving from Greek **Herakles,** the name of the son of
Zeus and Alkmene, famous for his feats of strength; of doubtful
origin, possibly meaning 'glory of Hera'.
Familiar forms: **Herk, Herkie.**

Hereward (m)
From Old English meaning 'army' + 'protection', it is best known as
the name of Hereward the Wake, 11th-century Anglo-Saxon rebel
against William the Conqueror.

Herk familiar form of **Hercules.**

Herkie familiar form of **Hercules.**

Hermia (f)
Like **Hermione**, derived from the Greek name **Hermes.** It was the
name of one of the mortal heroines in Shakespeare's *A Midsummer
Night's Dream.*

Hermione (f) [her-my-on-ee]
From Greek, based on the name **Hermes**, the messenger of the gods,
it was the name of a daughter of Helen and Menelaus, in Greek
legend. Used for the name of characters by Shakespeare and by Sir
Walter Scott. Occasionally used in modern times, for example by the
actresses Hermione Gingold and, more recently, Hermione Baddeley.

Hernán see **Ferdinand.**

Hester variant form of **Esther.**

Hettie variant form of **Henrietta** or of **Hester.**

Hew Welsh form of **Hugh.**

Hilary (m and f)
From Latin meaning 'cheerful'. The Latin masculine form **Hilarius**
was the name of a 4th-century saint. In former times it was normally
a male name but since the late 19th century it has been commoner as
a female name (from the Latin **Hilaria**).
Variant form: **Hillary.**

Hilda (f)
Of Germanic origin, meaning 'battle', from the first part of several
German names (such as **Hildegard**). The 7th-century St Hilda

founded the abbey of Whitby in Northumbria. The name was popular, especially in the north of England, in the Middle Ages and again in the late 19th and early 20th centuries.

Hildred (f)
From Old English meaning 'battle' + 'counsel'.

Hillary variant form of **Hilary**.

Hiram (m)
Biblical, possibly from Hebrew meaning 'brother' + 'high', it was the name of a king of Tyre in the Old Testament. It was popular with Puritans in the 17th century and continued to be used in America.

Holly (f)
From the plant name. Popular in the 20th century, especially recently. It may have gained popularity from the character, Holly Forsyte, in *The Forsyte Saga* by John Galsworthy. It was also used by Scott Fitzgerald for the name of a character in *Tender is the Night* (1934).

Homer (m)
English form of the name of the Greek epic poet; of doubtful origin, it may possibly mean 'hostage'. Homer Simpson is a character in the cult TV cartoon *The Simpsons*.

Honor (f) [on-or]
From Latin **Honoria**, female form of **Honorius**, from *honor* 'honour'. Popular with Puritans in the 17th century.
Other forms: **Honour, Honora, Onóra** (Irish Gaelic).
Familiar form: **Nora**.

Honora variant form of **Honor**.
Familiar form: **Nora**.

Honour variant form of **Honor**.

Hope (f)
It was brought into use (for both sexes) by the Puritans in the 17th century, referring to the Christian virtue. Now normally a female name.

Horace (m)
From the Roman family name, known from the poet Horace
(Quintus Horatius Flaccus), it was popular in the 19th century.
Variant form: **Horatio** [horayshio] (the first name of Admiral Lord
Nelson).

Hortense French form of **Hortensia**.

Hortensia (f)
Female form of the Latin family name **Hortensius**, possibly from
hortus 'garden', it has been used rarely in Britain.
Variant form: **Hortense** (French [ortons]).

Howard (m)
From the surname, the family name of the Dukes of Norfolk. The
origin is obscure.

Howell variant form of **Hywel**.

Hubert (m)
Norman-French of Germanic origin, meaning 'mind, heart' +
'bright'. It was popular in the Middle Ages and again in the late 19th
century. The 8th-century St Hubert was the patron saint of hunters.

Hugh (m)
Norman-French of Germanic origin, meaning 'mind, heart'. It is used
in Ireland and in the Highlands of Scotland as an anglicized form of
several Gaelic names such as **Aodh** (Irish Gaelic [ay]) and **Uisdean**
(Scottish Gaelic [ooshteean]).
Other forms: **Hugo** (Latinized), **Hew, Huw** (both Welsh).
Familiar forms: **Hughie, Shug, Shuggie** (both Scottish).

Humbert (m)
Norman-French of Germanic origin meaning 'warrior' + 'bright'. It
has never been popular in Britain. Humbert Humbert was the name
of the narrator of Vladimir Nabokov's novel *Lolita* (1955) and his
personality has done nothing to increase its popularity.

Humph familiar form of **Humphrey**.

Humphrey (m)
Norman-French of Germanic origin, meaning 'warrior' + 'peace',
though an Old English form was in use before the Conquest. It has
been used in Ireland as an anglicized form of Gaelic **Amhlaoibh**
[ow-leev].
Variant form: **Humphry.**
Familiar forms: **Humph, Humpo.**

Hunter (m)
From the (mainly Scottish) surname, itself originally an occupational
name. Hunter S Thomson is an American author.

Huw variant form of **Hugh.**

Hy familiar form of **Hyman.**

Hyacinth (f)
Now used occasionally as a female name, from the flower name.
Formerly a male name, being the name of several early saints, and
based on the name of the beautiful youth in Greek mythology. See
also **Jacinta.**

Hyam variant form of **Hyman.**

Hyman (m)
A Jewish name, from Hebrew meaning 'life'.
Other forms: **Chaim** (Hebrew [khyme]), **Hyam.**
Familiar forms: **Hymie, Hy.**

Hymie familiar form of **Hyman.**

Hywel (m) [how-el]
From Welsh meaning 'eminent' or 'conspicuous'. Used since the
Middle Ages, it is a popular 20th-century name in Wales and
common as a second name in north-west England.
Variant forms: **Hywell, Howell.**

Iain (m) [eean]
Scottish Gaelic form of **John**. Especially in the variant form **Ian**, it has
become popular outside Scotland in the 20th century.
Variant forms: **Ian, Ean.**

Ibby familiar form of **Isabel.**

Ida (f) [eye-da]
Norman-French of Germanic origin, probably meaning 'hard work'.
It was popular in the Middle Ages and again in the late 19th century,
partly because of its use as the name of the main character in
Tennyson's *The Princess,* and possibly because of Gilbert and
Sullivan's opera *Princess Ida.* It is sometimes used as an anglicized
form of Irish Gaelic **Íde.**

Íde (f) [eed-ya]
From Irish Gaelic, of uncertain origin, it was the name of a 6th-
century saint. Sometimes anglicized as **Ita** [eye-ta] or **Ida** [eye-da].

Idris (m)
From Welsh meaning 'lord' + 'fiery, ardent'. Popular in the Middle
Ages and again from the late 19th century.

Idwal (m) [id-wal]
From Welsh meaning 'master' + 'rampart'.

Ieuan (m) [yoo-an]
Welsh form of **John.**

Ifor (m)
Welsh name of unknown origin. Sometimes used as a Welsh form of
Ivor.

Ignatius (m) [ignayshus]
From a Roman family name of uncertain origin, it was the name of
several saints, notably the Spanish St Ignatius Loyola (1491-1556),
founder of the Society of Jesus (the Jesuits). Now occasionally used
by Roman Catholics. Other form: **Inigo** (Spanish; it was borne by the
17th-century architect Inigo Jones and his father).

Ike familiar form of **Isaac**.

Ilean, Ileen, Ileene, Ilene variant forms of **Eileen**.

Ilona (f)
Hungarian form of **Helen**, occasionally used in the English-speaking world.

Ilse German form of **Elizabeth**.

Immanuel variant form of **Emmanuel**.

Imogen (f) [imojen]
First used as the name of a character in Shakespeare's *Cymbeline*, where it was a misprint for **Innogen**, a name of Celtic origin, probably meaning 'girl, maiden'.

Ina (f) [eye-na, ee-na]
Familiar form of names with this ending, such as **Christina, Georgina, Wilhelmina**. Popular in Scotland until recently, especially for female names derived from male ones.

Inez Spanish form of **Agnes**.

Inge (f) [ing-a]
Familiar form of German **Ingeborg** (meaning 'protection of Ing'), it is occasionally used in the English-speaking world.

Ingrid (f)
Old Norse from the name of the fertility god 'Ing' + 'fair, beautiful'. Commonly used in Scandinavia and made popular in mid 20th-century Britain by the Swedish film actress Ingrid Bergman.

Inigo see **Ignatius**.

Innogen see **Imogen**.

Iomhar Scottish Gaelic form of **Ivor**.

Iona (f) [eye-ona]
The name is popular in Scotland after the small Hebridean island, off
the coast of Mull, where St Columba set up a monastery in the 6th
century, spreading Christianity to parts of Scotland. The
name is from a Latin form of its Gaelic name *I*, itself deriving from
Old Norse *ey* meaning 'island'.

Ira (m) [eye-ra]
Biblical, from Hebrew meaning 'watchful'; in the Old Testament it
was the name of one of King David's captains (2 Samuel (23:26). It
was used by the Puritans in the 17th century and is now more
popular in the USA than in Britain.

Irene (f) [eye-reen, eye-ree-ni (now rather old-fashioned)]
Latin, from Greek meaning 'peace', it was the name of a goddess of
peace in Greek mythology. Much used in early Christian times, it was
popular in the English-speaking world in the late 19th and early 20th
centuries.

Iris (f)
From Greek meaning 'rainbow', it was the name of a goddess in
Greek mythology who brought messages from gods to men along a
rainbow. It is also associated with the plant name and became
popular in Britain, along with other flower names, in the late 19th
century. A famous bearer of the name is the novelist Iris Murdoch.

Irma (f)
Familiar form of various German names, such as **Irmgard**, it is now
also used in the English-speaking world.

Irving (m)
From the Scottish surname, itself based on a place name in Dumfries-
shire. In Jewish families it is sometimes used as an anglicized from of
Israel, as in the case of the song-writer Irving Berlin (1888-1989), born
Israel Baline.

Isa familiar form of **Isabella**.

Isaac (m)
Biblical, probably from Hebrew meaning 'laugh', in the Old

Testament it was the name of the son of Abraham and Sarah (Genesis
21). Regarded as a Jewish name in the Middle Ages, it became
popular among Puritans in the 17th century. A famous bearer of the
name at that time was Sir Isaac Newton, the mathematician and
philosopher. It is now once more used mainly by Jews.
Variant form: Izaak (as in Izaak Walton, author of *The Compleat
Angler* (1653)).
Familiar forms: Ike, Zak.

Isabel (f)
Spanish form of Elizabeth, it came to France and then to England,
becoming popular, especially in Scotland in the late 19th century.
Other forms: Isobel (mainly Scottish), Isabella, Iseabail (Scottish
Gaelic [eeshepal], sometimes anglicized as Ishbel).
Familiar forms: Isa, Belle, Bella, Ibby, Izzie, Ella, Tibbie.

Isadora variant form of Isidora.

Isaiah (m)
Biblical, from Hebrew meaning 'God is salvation', it was the name of
one of the great prophets of the Old Testament. Though popular for a
time among Purtians in the 17th century, it is generally regarded as a
Jewish name. A well-known bearer in modern times is the
philosopher Isaiah Berlin.

Iseabail Scottish Gaelic form of Isabel.

Ishbel see Isabel.

Isidora (f)
Female form of Isidore.
Variant form: Isadora (given some prominence in the early 20th
century by the American dancer Isadora Duncan (1878-1927).

Isidore (m)
Old French and Latin from Greek meaning 'gift of Isis', it was used
by early Christians and was the name of several saints. It was later
used by Spanish Jews and is now considered a Jewish name.
Familiar form: Izzie.

Isla (f) [eye-la]
From a Scottish place name, either from the Hebridean island of
Islay (usually pronounced as above) or from the river in Angus and
Perthshire or that in Banffshire. Isla St Clair is a Scottish singer and
TV personality, well-known in the 1970s.

Isobel variant form of **Isabel**.

Israel (m)
Biblical, from Hebrew meaning 'struggle with God', it was the name
given to Jacob after he had struggled with an angel (Genesis 32: 28).
Always a popular Jewish name, it was also used by Puritans in the
17th century.
Familiar forms: **Izzie, Issie**.

Ita anglicized form of Irish Gaelic **Íde**.

Ivan (m) [eye-van, ee-van]
Slav form of **John**.

Ivar variant form of **Ivor**.

Ivor (m)
From Old Norse meaning 'yew, bow' + 'warrior', it is sometimes
used as an anglicization of the Welsh **Ifor**.
Other forms: **Ivar, Iomhar** (Scottish Gaelic [eevar].
Familiar form: **Ivy** (Scottish).
Ivy (f)
From the plant name. With other plant names it was popular in the
late 19th and early 20th centuries. See also **Ivor**.

Izaak variant form of **Isaac**.

Izzie familiar form of **Isabel, Isidore, Israel**.

Jacinta (f)
Spanish form of **Hyacinth**, now also used in the English-speaking
world.
Variant form: **Jacintha**.

Jack (m)
Familiar form of **John**, now a popular name in its own right. Derived from Middle English Jankin. It is sometimes regarded as an English form of French **Jacques**, though there is no connection between the names. See also **Jake** amd **Jock**.
Familiar forms: **Jackie, Jacky** (though these are now more commonly female names).

Jackie, Jacky familiar forms of **Jack, John, Jacqueline**.

Jackson (m)
From the surname, meaning 'son of Jack'.

Jacob (m)
Biblical, from Hebrew of uncertain origin, it was the name of the son of Isaac and Rebecca, who tricked his twin brother Esau out of his inheritance (Genesis 25:25-34). His sons gave their names to the twelve tribes of Israel. It remains a popular Jewish name. Latin forms are **Jacobus** and **Jacomus** (from which derives **James**).
Familiar form: **Jake** (also used as a name in its own right).

Jacqueline (f)
Female form of French **Jacques** and thus of **James** and **Jacob**. Very popular, especially since the 1960s, possibly influenced by Jacqueline Kennedy, wife of the US President J F Kennedy.
Variant form: **Jaqueline**.
Familiar forms: **Jackie, Jacky, Jacqui**.
Jacques see **James**.

Jacquetta (f)
Female form of **James** (from French **Jacques**).

Jacqui familiar form of **Jacqueline**.

Jade (f)
From the name of the precious stone, it has gained considerable popularity since the 1970s.

Jaime (m and f)
A Spanish and Portuguese form of **James**, in recent decades it has been used also as a female name.

Jaimie variant form of **Jamie**, mainly a female name.

Jake (m)
Familiar form of **Jack, Jacob**, also used as a name in its own right. Jake and Elwood were the Blues Brothers of the 1970s film musical.

James (m)
From Latin **Jacomus**, a variant form of **Jacobus** (see also **Jacob**), it is used as the English form of the name of two of Christ's disciples. Popular in the Middle Ages when many went on a pilgrimage to the shrine of St James at Compostela in Spain. Especially popular in Scotland, where it was the name of seven Stewart kings, two of them also kings of the United Kingdom. When James VII and II was ousted at the Glorious Revolution of 1688 the supporters of the Stewart dynasty came to be known as the Jacobites, from the Latin form of the name. It is now a very popular name throughout the English-speaking world. See also **Jaime**.
Other forms: **Seumas** (Scottish Gaelic), **Séamas** (Irish Gaelic), **Hamish** (anglicized form of Scottish Gaelic address form **Sheumais**), **Jacques** (French [zhak]; in Shakespeare's *As You Like It* it is pronounced [jaykwez]).
Familiar forms: **Jim, Jimmy, Jimmie, Jem, Jay, Jamie** (Scottish, though now also used elsewhere as a female name).

Jamesina (f) [james-eye-na]
Rather old-fashioned female form of **James**, formerly popular in Scotland.
Familiar form: **Ina**.

Jamie (m and f)
Scottish familiar form of **James**, now also used as a female name.
Variant form: **Jaimie** (mainly female).

Jan (m and f)
Familiar form of **John**, or Dutch, Scandinavian, Polish form [pronounced 'yan']; also familiar of form of **Janet, Jane**.

109

Jane (f)
Female form of John, from Old French **Jehane**. Very popular in the 19th century, when it was the name of the novelist Jane Austen and of the principal character in Charlotte Bronte's novel *Jane Eyre*. Often combined with other names, as in **Mary Jane, Emma Jane**.
Other forms: **Jayne, Janice, Janis, Janine** ([janeen], probably from French **Jeannine**), **Siobhán** (Irish Gaelic [she-vawn], **Sian** (Welsh [shahn]); see also **Janet, Jean, Joan, Joanna, Joanne, Johanna**.
Familiar forms: **Janey, Janie, Jan**.

Janet (f)
Female form of John, from French **Jeannette**, which is also used in Britain. Both names were until recently very popular in Scotland.
Other forms: **Janette, Janetta, Janice, Janis, Seònaid** (Scottish Gaelic [shaw-natch], often anglicized as **Shona**), **Sinéad** (Irish Gaelic [she-nayd]; see also **Jane, Jean, Jeanne, Joan, Joanna, Joanne, Johanna**.
Familiar forms: **Jan, Netta, Nettie, Jenny, Jennie, Jessie** (last three Scottish).

Janey familiar form of **Jane**.

Janice variant form of **Jane** or **Janet**.

Janie familiar form of **Jane**.

Janine variant form of **Jane**.

Janis variant form of **Jane** or **Janet**. Janis Joplin was a well-known American singer in the 1960s and 70s.

Japheth (m)
Biblical, from Hebrew meaning 'enlargement', in the Old Testament (Genesis 9, 10) Japheth was one of the sons of Noah. The name was used by the Puritans in the 17th century, but is now rare.

Jaqueline variant form of **Jacqueline**.

Jarvis (m)
From the surname, itself from the first name **Gervase**.

Jasmine (f)
From the plant name, coming into use with so many others in the late 19th century. From Persian via Old French.
Variant forms: **Yasmin, Yasmine.**

Jason (m)
From Greek, probably meaning 'heal', it was the name of the hero in Greek mythology who led the Argonauts, sailing in search of the Golden Fleece. It is also found in the New Testament (Acts 17:5-9, Romans 16:21), where it is probably a version of the Hebrew name **Joshua.** It was therefore popular with Puritans in the 17th century. It enjoyed a considerable vogue from the 1950s to the 1980s, partly due to its being used as the name of several characters in well-known television series and films.

Jasper (m)
Of uncertain origin, possibly from Persian meaning 'treasure-keeper', it was traditionally the name of one of the 'Three Wise Men' who brought gifts to the infant Christ. The Dutch form **Caspar** and occasionally the French **Gaspard [gaspar]** are also found. There does not seem to be any connection with the gemstone jasper.

Jay (m, occasionally f)
Familiar form of **James** and other names beginning with letter 'J'. Also used as a name in its own right.

Jayne variant form of **Jane.**

Jean (f)
Originally Scottish form of **Jane** or **Joan,** it is now used throughout the English-speaking world.
Other form: **Sìne** (Scottish Gaelic [sheena], anglicized as **Sheena**); see also **Jane, Jeanne, Joan, Joanna, Joanne, Johanna.**
Familiar form: **Jeanie.**

Jeanette variant form of **Jeannette.**

Jeanne (f)
Female form of **Jean,** French form of **John,** also used in the English-

speaking world. A famous bearer was Jeanne d'Arc (Joan of Arc), medieval French heroine. See also **Jane**, **Jean**, **Joan**.

Jeannette (f)
French diminutive female form of **John**; see also **Janet**, **Jeanne**.
Variant form; **Jeanette**.
Familiar form: **Jinty** (Scottish).

Jed familiar form of **Gerald** or **Gerard**.

Jeff familiar form of **Jeffrey**.

Jefferson (m)
From the surname, itself meaning 'son of Jeffrey'. In the USA it is often given in honour of Thomas Jefferson (1743-1826), who drafted the Declaration of Independence in 1776 and became the third president.

Jeffrey variant form of **Geoffrey**.

Jem familiar form of **James**, **Jeremy**.

Jemima (f)
Biblical, from Hebrew meaning 'dove', it was the name of one of the daughters of Job (Job 42:14). It was popular with Puritans in the 17th century and remained so until the 19th century. Sometimes used as a female form of **James**. Now rare, but remembered from *The Tale of Jemima Puddleduck* by Beatrix Potter.
Familiar form: **Mima**.

Jemma variant form of **Gemma**.

Jen familiar form of **Jennifer**.

Jenifer variant form of **Jennifer**.

Jenna variant form of **Jenny**.

Jenni familiar form of **Jennifer**.

Jennie variant form of **Jenny**.

Jennifer (f)
Of Celtic origin, a Cornish form of **Guinevere,** in Arthurian legend
the wife of King Arthur. Became popular in the 20th century
throughout the English-speaking world.
Variant form: **Jenifer**
Familiar forms: **Jenny, Jenni, Jen.**

Jenny (f)
Variant form of **Janet, Jennifer,** also used as a name in its own right.
Variant forms: **Jennie,Jenna** (name of a character in the television
soap opera *Dallas*).

Jep familiar form of **Jepson**.

Jepson (m)
From the surname, itself from a medieval familiar form of **Geoffrey**.
Familiar form: **Jep**.

Jeremiah (m)
Biblical, from Hebrew meaning 'God-appointed', it was the name of
the Old Testament prophet whose prophecies are found in 'Jeremiah'
and in 'Lamentations'. It was popular with Puritans in the 17th
century, and is still found in Ireland, where it has been used as an
anglicized form of **Diarmaid**. The English form **Jeremy** has been
much used this century and continues to enjoy popularity.
Familiar forms: **Jerry, Jem.**

Jeremy see **Jeremiah**.

Jerome (m)
From from the French form of Greek **Hyeronimos** meaning 'holy' +
'name'. The 4th-century St Jerome was responsible for translating the
Bible into Latin. The name became popular in England, helped by
Jerome K Jerome and his *Three Men in a Boat* (1889).
Familiar form: **Jerry**.

Jerrard variant form of **Gerard**.

Jerry familiar form of **Gerald, Gerard, Jeremy, Jerome**.

Jess familiar form of **Jessica, Jessie**.

Jessamine (f)
Variant form of **Jasmine**.
Variant form: **Jessamy**.

Jesse (m) [jesi]
Biblical from Hebrew, probably meaning 'gift', it was the name of the father of King David (1 Samuel 16). Popular with Puritans in the 17th century, it has remained so in the USA, where famous (or infamous) bearers include the 19th-century outlaw Jesse James and, more recently, Jesse Jackson, black American civil rights leader.

Jessica (f)
Possibly based on a Biblical name, it was used by Shakespeare for the name of Shylock's daughter in *The Merchant of Venice*.
Familiar form: **Jess, Jessie**.

Jessie (f)
Familiar form of **Janet, Jessica;** also used as a name in its own right. Formerly popular in Scotland; its decline may be partly due to the use of the word in Scots to refer to an effeminate man.
Familiar form: **Jess**.

Jesus see **Joshua**.

Jethro (m)
Biblical, from Hebrew meaning 'excellence', it was the name of the father-in-law of Moses (Exodus 3:1, 4:18). Popular with Puritans in the 17th century, it was less used in later times. A famous bearer was the 18th-century agricultural reformer Jethro Tull; his name was adopted by a late 20th-century rock group, from whom the name enjoyed a revival in the 1970s.

Jetta (f)
Based on the mineral jet, with Latin ending.

Jewel (f)
The word for a precious stone, used as a name, especially in the USA.
Variant form: **Jewell**.

Jill (f)
Familiar form of **Jillian, Gillian**, also used as a name in its own right.

Jillian variant form of **Gillian**.

Jillie, Jilly familiar forms of **Jillian, Gillian**.

Jim, Jimmy, Jimmie familiar forms of **James**, also occasionally used as names in their own right.

Jinny familiar form of **Virginia**.

Jinty Scottish familiar form of **Jeannette**.

Jo familiar form of **Joanna, Joanne, Johanna, Josephine** and occasionally of **Joseph**; compare **Joe**.

Joan (f)
Female form of **John**, from Old French **Johanne**. It was popular in the Middle Ages and again in the 20th century, possibly partly because of George Bernard Shaw's play *St Joan*, Joan of Arc being the usual English name for the French medieval heroine Jeanne d'Arc. See also **Jane, Janet, Joanna, Joanne, Johanna**.
Other form; **Seònag** (Scottish Gaelic [shaw-nack]).
Familiar form: **Joanie**.

Joanna (f)
Female form of **John**, from Greek via Latin; see also **Jane, Janet, Joan, Joanne, Johanna**.
Familiar form; **Jo**.

Joanne (f) [jo-ann]
Female form of **John**, from Old French **Johanne**; see also **Joan**.
Familiar form: **Jo**.

Jocasta (f)
In Greek legend, the name of the mother of Oedipus, King of Thebes, who also became his wife, with tragic consequences.

Jock (m)
Scottish familiar form of **John**, probably a variant of **Jack**. Used to refer to any Scotsman or, since World War I, to a soldier in one of the Scottish regiments.
Variant form: **Jockie**.

Jocelyn (m and f)
From a surname of Norman-French origin, probably based on the name of a Germanic tribe. Originally a male name, it is now more usually female; sometimes thought to be connected with **Joyce**.
Familiar forms: **Jos, Joss**

Jodie, Jody familiar forms of **Judith**, also used as names in their own right.

Joe familiar form of **Joseph**; compare **Jo**.

Joel (m)
Biblical, from two Hebrew words, both meaning 'God'. The name is frequently found in the Bible and is the name of one of the books of the Old Testament. Always a Jewish name, it was used by the Puritans in the 17th century.

Joey familiar form of **Joseph**.

Johanna (f)
Female form of **John**, from medieval Latin; see also **Joanna**.
Familiar form: **Jo**.

John (m)
From Hebrew meaning 'God is gracious', it was an important name in early Christian times, being the name of John the Baptist, of one of Christ's disciples, and of John the Evangelist, a 1st-century Greek now thought to be the author of the fourth gospel. It was the name of many other saints and of 23 popes. For centuries it was the most popular male first name throughout the English-speaking world but,

like other traditional names, it has recently lost ground, though some other forms, such as **Ian**, have gained.
Other forms: **Jon**; see also **Iain, Seán, Evan, Ieuan, Ivan, Jan**.
Familiar forms: **Johnny, Johnnie, Seonaidh** (Scottish Gaelic [shonee]; see also **Jack, Jock**.

Jolyon variant form of **Julian**. Rare, but remembered from Jolyon Forsyte, character in *The Forsyte Saga* by John Galsworthy.

Jon familiar form of **Jonathan**; variant form of **John**.

Jonah (m)
Biblical, from Hebrew meaning 'dove'. In the Old Testament, the Book of Jonah tells of Jonah being thrown overboard in a storm and swallowed by a whale.

Jonathan, Jonathon (m)
Biblical, from Hebrew meaning 'gift of God', it is found in the Old Testament, especially as the name of the son of Saul who became the friend of David (1 Samuel 31; 2 Samuel 1 17-26), giving rise to the literary expression 'David and Jonathan' as a symbol of true friendship. It was popular with Puritans in the 17th century. A well-known 18th-century bearer was the Irish writer Jonathan Swift, author of *Gulliver's Travels*.
Familiar forms: **Jon, Jonnie, Jonny, Jonty**.

Jonquil (f)
From the flower name, used like so many others in recent times.

Jonty familiar form of **Jonathan**.

Jordan (m and f)
From the name of the river in the Middle East, from which water was brought back for baptism in the Middle Ages. It was therefore used as a male first name, and then as a surname, which is probably the origin of the modern first name. It is now used as a female as well as a male name.

Jos familiar form of **Jocelyn, Joseph, Joshua**.

Joseph (m)
Biblical, from Hebrew meaning 'God will add'. Joseph was the twelfth son of Jacob and Rachel, and was sold into slavery by his jealous brothers (Genesis 37). In the New Testament it was the name of the husband of the Virgin Mary, and of Joseph of Arimathaea, who was said to have buried Christ after the Crucifixion. Mainly a Jewish name in the Middle Ages, it became popular with Puritans in the 17th century, and remained so until the mid 20th century.
Familiar forms: **Joe, Jo, Joey, Jos.**

Josepha (f)
Female form of **Joseph**, less popular than **Josephine**.

Josephine (f)
Female form of Joseph, from the French female form **Josèphe**, it became popular in the 19th century after the first wife of Napoleon Bonaparte.
Familiar forms: **Jo, Josie, Posy, Posie.**

Josh familiar form of **Joshua**.

Joshua (m)
Biblical, from Hebrew meaning 'God saves'; **Jesus** is another form of the same name. It was the name of the leader of the Israelites who followed Moses, and eventually led his people into the promised land. It became popular with Puritans in the 17th century, and remained so, especially in America.
Familiar forms: **Josh, Joss, Jos.**

Josie familiar form of **Josephine**.

Joss familiar form of **Jocelyn, Joshua.**

Joy (f)
From the word meaning 'happiness', it has been in use since the Middle Ages, becoming popular in the late 19th century.

Joyce (f, formerly m)
From a French form, **Joisse**, of **Jodocus**, the Latin form of the name of a 7th-century Breton saint. A male name in medieval times, it

survived only as a surname, but was revived as a female name in the 20th century, after modest use by Puritans in the 17th century.

Juanita (f) [hwa-nee-ta]
Female form of **Juan**, Spanish form of **John**, also used in English-speaking countries.

Judah, Judas see **Jude**.

Judd (m)
From the surname, itself a medieval familiar form of **Jordan**, used especially in the USA.

Jude (m)
Biblical, from Hebrew, probably meaning 'praise', familiar form of **Judah**, the name of one of the sons of Jacob, who gave his name to one of the twelve tribes of Israel (Genesis 29:35). The Greek form **Judas** is found in the New Testament, but has never been popular in view of its association with Judas Iscariot, the disciple who betrayed Christ. Christ had another disciple of this name, referred to as Jude in the Authorized Version, as in *The General Epistle of Jude*. The best-known literary bearer of the name is the hero of Thomas Hardy's *Jude the Obscure* (1895). See also **Judith**.
Other forms: **Yehuda, Yehudi** (both Hebrew).

Judith (f)
Biblical, from Hebrew meaning 'Jewess', it was the name of the wife of Esau in the Old Testament (Genesis 26:34) and the Apocrypha has *The Book of Judith*. Always a popular name among Jews, it has had spells of popularity in the English-speaking world generally, especially in the 18th century, and even more so in the 20th.
Familiar forms: **Jude, Judy, Judie, Judi, Jody, Jodie** (also used as names in their own right).

Jules (m and f)
French form of **Julius**; familiar form of **Julian** and of **Julia, Julie, Juliana**.

Julia (f)
Female form of **Julius**, it was the name of several early saints.

Popular since the 18th century, it has recently lost out to its French form **Julie**.
Other form: **Julie** (French).

Julian (m, formerly also f)
From Latin **Julianus**, the name of the Roman Emperor Julian the Apostate, who tried to turn the Empire away from Christianity. It was also the name of several saints. It was used as a female as well as a male name in the Middle Ages, but pronounced **Gillian** and in this form it survives. A medieval example is the Blessed Julian of Norwich in the late 15th century. As a male name it continues to be used; see also **Jolyon**.
Familiar form: **Jules**.

Juliana (f)
Female form of Latin **Julianus**. Used in Britain from the 18th century, it is more popular in other European countries; it is the name of a recent Queen of the Netherlands. See also **Julia, Julie**.
Familiar form: **Jules**.

Julie (f)
French form of **Julia**. It has become more popular than other forms of the name. May have gained popularity in the 1960s and 70s from the actresses Julie Harris and Julie Andrews.
Familiar form: **Jules**.

Juliet (f)
From the Italian **Giulietta** or French **Juliette** familiar forms of **Julia**, best-known from Juliet Capulet, heroine of Shakespeare's *Romeo and Juliet*.

Julius (m)
From the Roman family name, well-known from the Roman leader Caius Julius Caesar. It was the name of two popes (in the 4th and 15th centuries). The derivative form **Julian** is much more popular in Britain, but Julius is used among Jews (possibly as a substitute for various Hebrew names beginning with the same sound), and in West Indian families.

June (f)
The month used as a name, it has been popular during the 20th century.

Justin (m)
From the Latin name Justinus, from *justus* meaning 'just'. It was formerly rather rare, but has enjoyed great popularity since the 1970s throughout the English-speaking world.

Justina see Justine.

Justine (f)[justeen]
French female form of **Justin**, now more popular than the Latin form **Justina** [justeena], probably influenced by Lawrence Durrell's novel *Justine* (1960), part of his Alexandria Quartet.

Kaety see Kate.

Kai (m) [rhymes with 'pie' or 'pay']
Welsh form of **Caius**.

Kane (m)
Probably from Irish Gaelic **Cáthair** meaning 'warrior'.

Kar familiar form of Karen.

Kara variant form of Cara.

Karen (f)
Danish familiar form of **Catherine**, introduced into the USA by Danish parents. It has enjoyed great popularity in Britain as well as North America in the second half of the 20th century.
Variant forms: **Carren, Karin** (Swedish).
Familiar forms: **Kar, Kaz.**

Karl variant form of Carl.

Kat familiar form of Kate, Katherine, Katarina, Katrina.

Katarina Swedish form of Catherine.

Kate (f)
Familiar form of **Catherine**, it is now very popular as a name in its
own right. It is the name of the main female character in
Shakespeare's *The Taming of the Shrew* (made into a musical comedy
with the title *Kiss me Kate*).
Variant forms: **Katie, Katy, Katey, Kaety** (all now used as names in
their own right).

Kath familiar form of **Katharine, Katherine** (see **Catherine**).

Katharine, Katherine, Katherin variant forms of **Catherine**.

Kathie, Kathy familiar forms of **Katharine, Katherine** (see
Catherine).

Kathleen Irish form of **Catherine**.

Kathryn variant form of **Catherine**.

Katie see **Kate**.

Katrina variant form of **Catriona** (see **Catherine**)

Katrine (f) [katrin]
Variant form of **Catherine**, or taken from the name of a Scottish loch
(from a Celtic root of doubtful origin).

Katy see **Kate**.

Kay (f and m)
Familiar form of **Catherine**, used as a name in its own right. Made
popular in the mid 20th century by the actress Kay Kendall.
Formerly also a male name, of uncertain Celtic origin, possibly based
on Latin **Gaius** (see **Caius**). In Arthurian legend it was the name of
one of the Knights of the Round Table.
Variant form: **Kaye**.

Kaz familiar form of **Karen**.

Keir (m)
From the Scottish surname, itself a variant of Kerr. It has sometimes
been given in honour of (James) Keir Hardie (1856-1915), Scottish
Labour leader.

Keiran variant form of **Kieran**.

Keith (m)
From the Scottish surname, itself based on a place name in East
Lothian. Like some other Scottish surnames, it has become popular
throughout the English-speaking world.

Kelley, Kellie variant forms of **Kelly**.

Kelly (m and f)
From the Irish surname, in Irish Gaelic Ó Ceallaigh, from **Ceallach**,
possibly meaning 'visitor of churches'. Now also used as a female
name, especially in Australia, where it may be a variant form of
Kylie.
Variant forms: **Kellie, Kelley**.

Kelvin (m)
From the name of a Scottish river, a tributary of the Clyde. The use of
the name may have been influenced by Lord Kelvin (William
Thomson 1824-1907), Irish-born Scottish scientist.

Ken familiar form of **Kenneth** and of other names beginning thus,
such as **Kendall, Kenton**.

Kendall (m)
From the surname, itself based on Kendal in Cumbria (meaning
'valley of the river Kent'), or possibly on Kendale in Humberside
(from Old Norse meaning 'spring' + 'valley').

Kenina (f)
Female form of **Kenneth**, formerly quite common in the Highlands of
Scotland.
Variant form: **Kenna**.

Kennedy (m and f)
From the surname, itself from Irish Gaelic **Cinnéide** meaning 'head'
+ 'ugly'. Its use may have been influenced by John F Kennedy (1917-
63), 35th president of the USA. It is also occasionally used as a female
name.

Kenneth (m)
From two Celtic names: **Cinaed** meaning 'fire-born' and **Cainnech**
meaning 'handsome, fair', in modern Scottish Gaelic **Coinneach**
[kinyach]. The first king of the united Scots and Picts in the 9th
century was Kenneth Mac Alpin (Cinaed mac Alpín). The clan
Mackenzie takes its name from the Gaelic form and Kenneth is a
popular first name among its members. It remained largely a Scottish
name until the late 19th century but its use has since spread to other
parts of the English-speaking world. Kenneth Grahame, author of
The Wind in the Willows (1908) was Scottish in origin, but more
recently there have been prominent English bearers of the name, such
as the actors Kenneth More and Kenneth Williams.
Familiar forms: **Ken, Kenny**, sometimes used as names in their own
right as in the case of the Scottish footballer Kenny Dalglish.

Kent (m)
From the surname, itself derived from the English county name,
probably meaning 'border'. It is now popular as a first name,
especially in the USA and Canada. It is also used as a familiar form of
Kenton.

Kenton (m)
From the surname, itself derived from various place names of
different origins, the second element from Old English meaning
'settlement'.

Familiar forms: **Ken, Kent**.

Kenyon (m)
From the surname, itself from an old Lancashire place name, from
Old English meaning 'Ennion's mound'.
Familiar form: **Ken**.

Keri variant form of **Kerry**.

Kermit (m)
From Irish or Manx Gaelic, derived from **Diarmaid** (see **Dermot**), it
has been made prominent in recent years by Kermit the Frog in the
television *Muppet Show.*

Kerr (m)
From the Scottish and northern English surname, itself from a place-
name element, deriving from Old Norse meaning 'rough ground
with brushwood'. The theory that it derives from Gaelic *cèarr*
meaning 'left-handed' is doubtful.

Kerri, Kerrie familiar forms of **Kerry.**

Kerry (m and f)
Probably derived from the Irish county name, it has been used as a
first name, especially a female name, mainly in Australia and Britain.
Variant forms: **Kerrie, Kerri, Keri.**

Keturah (f)
Biblical, from Hebrew meaning 'incense', in the Old Testament it was
the name of the second wife of Abraham (Genesis 25:1). It was used
by the Puritans in the 17th century.

Kev familiar form of **Kevin**

Kevan variant form of **Kevin.**

Kevin (m)
From Irish Gaelic **Caoimhínn** [ke-veen], 'handsome, beloved' +
'born', it was the name of a 7th-century Irish saint. In the 20th
century it has become popular outside Ireland.
Variant form: **Kevan.**
Familiar forms: **Kev, Kevvie.**

Kez familiar form of **Kezia.**

Kezia (f)
Biblical, from Hebrew meaning 'cassia-tree', it was the name of one
of the daughters of Job (Job 42: 14). Popular in Black American
families.

Variant form: **Keziah.**
Familiar forms **Kizzie, Kiz, Kez.**

Kiaran variant form of **Kieran**

Kiera anglicized form of **Ciara.**

Kieran (m)
Anglicized form of Irish Gaelic **Ciarán** [kee-a-rawn], meaning 'little dark one'
Variant forms: **Kiaran, Kieren, Kieron, Keiran.**

Kilie variant form of **Kylie.**

Killian (m)
Anglicized form of Irish Gaelic **Cillian**, probably from *cill* meaning 'church'. It was the name of several early Irish saints.

Kim (f and m)
Familiar form of **Kimberley**, also used as a name in its own right. Originally a male name, now much commoner as a female one. The name of the main character in Rudyard Kipling's novel *Kim* (1901) was shortened from Kimball O'Hara.

Kimberley (f and m)
From the diamond-mining town in South Africa, which was the scene of fighting during the Boer War at the turn of the century. Thereafter it became popular for a time as a male name; later in the century it rose to prominence once more, but as a female name. The town was called after Lord Kimberley, whose surname is based on an English place name, derived from a personal name + 'wood, clearing.'
Variant form: **Kimberly.**
Familiar form: **Kim**; see also above.

King (m)
Either from the surname or from the word, it is popular in Black American families, probably partly in honour of Martin Luther King (1929-68), black civil rights leader.

Kingsley (m)
From the surname, itself from a place name, deriving from Old
English meaning 'king's wood'. Kingsley Amis (1922-) is an English
novelist.

Kirk (m)
From the Scottish and northern English surname, itself from Old
Norse meaning 'church'. It was brought to prominence in the mid
20th century by the film actor Kirk Douglas (Issur Danielovich
Demsky 1916-).

Kirsteen Scottish variant form of **Christine.**

Kirsten (f)
Scandinavian form of **Christine**, now used in English-speaking
countries. The form **Kirstin** has long been used in Scotland.

Kirsty, Kirstie Scottish variant forms of **Christine,** familiar forms of
Kirstin, now popular in other English-speaking countries.

Kit (m and f)
Familiar form of **Christopher** or of **Katherine, Catherine.**

Kitty, Kittie familiar forms of **Katherine, Catherine,** also used as
names in their own right.

Kiz familiar form of **Kezia.**

Kizzie familiar form of **Kezia.**

Konrad variant form of **Conrad.**

Krystal variant form of **Crystal.**

Krystle variant form of **Crystal.**

Kyle (m)
From the Scottish surname, itself from a place name, probably
deriving from Gaelic *caol* meaning 'narrow' (referring to a strait or
other narrow place).

Kylie (f)
Either from a Western Australian Aboriginal word meaning
'boomerang' or possibly simply a variant of **Kelly** or **Kyle**, it has
become very popular in Australia and is now used in other English-
speaking countries, perhaps partly due to the popularity of the
Australian singer and actress Kylie Minogue.
Variant form: **Kilie**.

Laban (m)
Biblical, from Hebrew meaning 'white'. In the Old Testament Laban
was the brother of Rebecca, wife of Isaac (Genesis 24:29). The name
was popular with Puritans in the 17th century.

Labhrainn Scottish Gaelic form of **Laurence**.

Lacey (m and f)
From the surname, itself of Norman-French origin, based on a place
name in Normandy. It is now used as a female as well as a male
name.
Variant form: **Lacy**.

Lachan see **Lachlan**.

Lachie familiar form of **Lachlan**.

Lachlan (m) [lakhlan]
From Scottish Gaelic **Lachlann** or **Lachann**, probably from *Lochlann*,
the Gaelic name for Norway (meaning 'land of the lakes'), it is used
mainly in the Highlands of Scotland.
Familiar form: **Lachie**.

Lacy variant form of **Lacey**.

Laelia (f)
From Latin meaning 'cheerful' or 'talkative'. The alternative spelling
is **Lelia** and it is the name of a 5th Century Irish Martyr. The name
can also serve as a short form of **Aurelia**.

Laetitia variant form of **Letitia**.

Lalage (f) [la-la-jee or la-la-gee]
From Greek meaning 'to babble, chatter', the name was used by the Latin poet Horace. A recent literary appearance was in *The French Lieutenant's Woman* by John Fowles (1969).
Familiar forms: **Lally, Lallie.**

Lambert (m)
Norman-French of Germanic origin, meaning 'land' + 'bright', it is now commoner as a surname.

Lana (f)
Probably a familiar form of **Alana**. It was the stage name of the film actress Lana Turner (1920-95).

Lance (m)
Either from Old Germanic meaning 'land' (and originally a shortened form of other names) or from Old French meaning 'lance'. Now also regarded as a familiar form of **Lancelot**, but much commoner than the full form.

Lancelot (m)
Of obscure, probably originally Celtic origin, in Arthurian legend, it was the name of one of the Knights of the Round Table, who became the lover of Queen Guinevere. More popular now in the familiar form **Lance**, but a modern bearer was Lancelot Hogben (1895-1975), English scientist who wrote books for the wider public.

Laoise see **Lucy.**

Lara (f)
Russian familiar form of **Larissa**, also used as a name in its own right. It was the name of one of the characters in Boris Pasternak's *Dr Zhivago* (1957).

Laraine (f)
Either a variant form of **Lorraine**, or else from French *la reine* meaning 'the queen'. Like other names beginning with la-, it has become popular with Black Americans.

Larissa (f)
Of uncertain origin, it was the name of an early Greek martyr.
Familiar form: **Lara**.

Larraine variant form of **Lorraine**.

Larry familiar form of **Laurence**.

Laura (f)
From Latin meaning 'bay-tree, laurel' (which was a symbol of victory
in ancient Rome). It was the name of the woman addressed by the
14th-century Italian poet Petrarch in his works.
Familiar form: **Laurie**, also used as a name in its own right.

Lauren (f)
Probably a female form of **Laurence**, it was brought to prominence in
the 1940s as the stage name of the American film actress Lauren
Bacall.
Variant form: **Loren** (which has also been used as a male name, a
variant of **Laurence**).

Laurence (m)
Norman-French, of Latin origin, meaning 'man from Laurentum', a
town near Rome (which may have got its name from abundance of
laurels in the area). See also **Lorcán**.
Other forms: **Lawrence** (formerly commoner as a surname),
Labhrainn (Scottish Gaelic [lowren].
Familiar forms: **Larry**, **Laurie**, **Lawrie** (especially in Scotland).

Laurie (m and f)
Familiar form of **Laurence**, **Laura**, also used a a name in its own
right.

Lavinia (f)
Of uncertain origin. In Roman mythology it was the name of the wife
of Aeneas.
Familiar forms: **Vinny**, **Vinnie**.

Lawrence variant form of **Laurence**.

Lawrie (m)
Familiar form of **Lawrence**, also used as a name in its own right..

Lea variant form of **Leah.**

Leah (f)
Biblical, from Hebrew, of uncertain origin, it was the name of the
wife of Jacob, who was tricked by her father Laban into marrying her
instead of her sister Rachel (Genesis 29:22-27). Always a common
Jewish name, it was also popular with Puritans in the 17th century.
Familiar forms: **Lea, Lee.**

Léan Irish Gaelic form of **Helen.**

Leanne variant form of **Liane.**

Lee (m and f)
From the surname, derived from Old English meaning 'wood,
clearing, meadow'. It was used as a male name after the Civil War in
the USA after the Confederate General Robert E Lee. Now also used
as a female name, sometimes as a familiar form of **Leah.**
Variant form: **Leigh.**

Lee-Ann variant form of **Liane.**

Leigh variant form of **Lee.**

Leigh-Anne variant form of **Liane.**

Leila (f)
From Arabic meaning 'of the night; dark-haired', it was used by Lord
Byron in his poems *The Giaour* (1813) and *Don Juan* (1819-24). In 1838
Lord Lytton used it for the chief character in his novel *Leila.*
Variant form: **Lila.**

Lelia see **Laelia**

Len familiar form of **Leonard** and also of **Lionel.**

Lena familiar form of **Helen.**

Lennie, Lenny familiar forms of **Leonard** and also of **Lionel**.

Lennox (m)
From the Scottish surname, itself from a place name, a district near Loch Lomond, the name probably connected with elm trees. Lennox Berkeley (1903-1989) was an English composer; Lennox Lewis is a heavyweight boxing champion.

Lenora, Lenore variant forms of **Eleanor**.

Leo (m) [lee-oh]
From Latin meaning 'lion', it was the name of many early Christian saints and popes.
Variant form: **Leon** (popular in Jewish families).

Leona (f)
Female form of **Leo**; see also **Léonie**.

Leonard m [lenard]
Norman-French of Germanic origin, meaning 'lion' + 'strong, brave', it was the name of a 5th-century Frankish saint.
Familiar forms: **Len, Lennie, Lenny.**

Léonie (f)
French female form of **Leo**, also used in English-speaking countries; see also **Leona**.

Leonora (f)
From the Italian form of **Eleanor**, it is the name of the heroine of several operas, including *Fidelio* by Beethoven.
Familiar forms: **Nora, Nornie.**

Leopold (m)
Germanic meaning 'people + 'bold', it was used in late 19th-century Britain, when Queen Victoria named one of her sons after her uncle, King Leopold of the Belgians.

Leroy (m)
From Old French meaning 'the king', the name is now popular
among Black Americans.
Familiar form: **Roy.**

Les familiar form of **Leslie.**

Lesley see **Leslie.**

Leslie, Lesley (m and f)
From the Scottish surname, itself from a place names in
Aberdeenshire and Fife. **Leslie** is usually a male name, except in the
USA; it was made popular in the mid 20th century by the film actor
Leslie Howard, especially after his role in *Gone with the Wind* (1939).
The usual female form is **Lesley**, possibly influenced by Robert
Burns's poem 'Bonny Lesley'. The film actress Leslie Caron, however,
made this spelling more acceptable as a female form.
Familiar form: **Les** (sometimes used as a name in its own right, as in
the case of the Australian poet Les Murray).

Lester (m)
From the English surname, based on the place name Leicester, it was
popular throughout the English-speaking world in the mid 20th
century. Well-known bearers of the name were the Canadian prime
minister Lester Pearson and the English jockey Lester Piggott.

Letitia (f) [le-ti-sha]
From Latin **Laetitia** meaning 'gladness', anglicized as **Lettice**, all are
very rare, but the first and third had some currency in the 19th
century.
Familiar forms: **Letty, Lettie.**

Lettie, Letty familiar forms of **Letitia, Arlette.**

Levi (m)
Biblical, from Hebrew meaning 'joined, attached'. In the Old
Testament it was the name of one of the sons of Jacob and Leah
(Genesis 29:34). In the New Testament it was a name of the apostle
Matthew. It is mainly used in Jewish families.

Lew familiar form of **Lewis** or of **Llewellyn**.

Lewella variant form of **Llewella**.

Lewis (m)
Norman-French of Germanic origin, meaning 'fame' + 'warrior', as in the German form **Ludwig**. The Latin form **Ludovicus** was altered to **Clovis**, name of the Frankish leader who ruled over most of what is now France in the 6th century. The French form **Louis** was the name of 18 French kings (from the 8th to the 19th centuries); it has become popular also in the English-speaking world, especially in the USA. It is normally pronounced in the French way [loo-ee], but the Scottish writer Robert Louis Stevenson, who was usually known by his middle name, pronounced it [loo-is]. A famous bearer of the Lewis form was Lewis Carroll, pen-name of Charles Lutwidge Dodgson, author of *Alice in Wonderland* (1865); the name Lewis was adapted from his middle name. In the USA Louis Armstrong was a famous jazz trumpeter of the mid 20th century. **Lewis** is used in Wales as an anglicized form of **Llewellyn**, in Ireland for Irish Gaelic **Laoiseach** and **Lughaidh**, and in Scotland occasionally after the place name (the Hebridean Isle of Lewis).
Familiar forms: **Lou, Louie** [from the French pronunciation], **Lew**.

Lex familiar form of **Alexander**.

Lexie, Lexy familiar forms of **Alexandra, Alexis**.

Liam familiar form of **Uilliam**, Irish Gaelic form of **William**.

Liane (f)
Of uncertain origin, perhaps a familiar form of **Juliana**, it has become popular in recent decades, in many variant forms, some suggesting other origins.
Variant forms: **Lianne, Leanne, Lee-Ann, Leigh-Anne**.

Libby familiar form of **Elizabeth**.

Liese familiar form of **Elizabeth**.

Lil familiar form of **Lily, Lilian**.

Lila variant form of **Leila**.

Lilac (f)
From the plant name, occasionally used as a first name.

Lilian (f)
Either a familiar form of **Elizabeth** or from the flower name, it was popular in the early 20th century.
Variant form: **Lillian** (especially in N America).
Familiar form: **Lil**.

Lilias (f)
Scottish form of **Lilian** or **Lily**.
Variant form: **Lilllias**.

Lillian variant form of **Lilian**

Lillias variant form of **Lilias**.

Lily (f)
From the flower name, regarded by Christians as a symbol of purity. It may also have been a familiar form of **Elizabeth**, especially in former times.
Familiar form: **Lil**.

Lin familiar form of **Linda**.

Lincoln (m)
From the surname, itself from name of the English city. In the USA often given in honour of Abraham Lincoln, 16th president.

Linda (f)
Probably originally a familiar form of various names, such as **Belinda**, with this ending, or may be from *linda*, feminine form of Spanish for pretty. Very popular in the middle part of the 20th century, reaching a peak in the 1950s.
Familiar forms: **Lindie, Lindy, Lin** (see also **Lyn**).

Lindsay (m and f)
From the Scottish surname, itself from an English place name,
probably meaning 'island of Lincoln'. Originally a male name, it is
now much commoner as a female name.
Variant form: Lindsey.

Lindy familiar form of **Linda**.
Linette variant form of **Lynette**.

Linus (m)
From Greek (via Latin), of uncertain origin. Used in the USA and
known in Britain from the character in the *Peanuts* strip cartoon.

Lionel (m)
Ultimately from Latin meaning 'little lion', it may have come through
the French form Léon.
Familiar forms: Len, Lennie, Lenny.

Lis familiar form of **Felicity**.

Lisa familiar form of **Elizabeth**, also used as a name in its own right.

Lisbeth variant form of **Elizabeth**.

Lisette familiar form of **Elizabeth**.

Liss familiar form of **Felicity**.

Lissa familiar form of **Felicity, Melissa**.

Lissie familiar form of **Felicity**.

Livy familiar form of **Olivia**.

Liz, Liza, Lizzie, Lizzy familiar forms of **Elizabeth**, occasionally used
as names in their own right.

Llewella (f)
Female form of Llewellyn.
Variant forms: Lewella; see also Louella.

Llewellyn (m) [hloo-ell-in]
Modern form of Welsh **Llywelyn**, of uncertain origin but possibly
from Welsh meaning 'leader' or from a word meaning 'lion'.
Familiar form: **Lew**.

Lloyd (m) [loyd, Welsh hloyd]
From Welsh meaning 'grey'.
Variant form: **Loyd**.

Llywelyn see Llewellyn.

Logan (m)
From the Scottish surname, itself from a place name in Ayrshire,
derived from Gaelic meaning 'hollow'.

Lois (f) [low-iss or loyce]
Biblical, possibly of Greek origin, in the New Testament it was the
name it was the name of the grandmother of Timothy (2 Timothy
1:5). Lois Lane was Superman's girlfriend.

Lola (f)
Originally a familiar form of **Dolores**, now used as a name in its own
right. A famous bearer was Lola Montez, stage name of an Irish
dancer, Marie Gilbert (1818-61), who had affairs with several famous
Europeans of her time, including King Ludwig I of Bavaria.
Familiar form: **Lolita**, also used as a name in its own right, especially
in America, though it has lost popularity since the publication of
Vladimir Nabokov's novel *Lolita* (1958/9), telling the story of an
affair between a middle-aged professor and a 12-year-old girl.

Loraine variant form of **Lorraine**.

Lorcán (m) [lor-can]
From Irish Gaelic meaning 'silent' or 'fierce'. Sometimes anglicized as
Laurence, although the names have no connection.

Loren see Lauren.

Lorn variant form of **Lorne**.

Lorna (f)
Invented by R D Blackmore for the heroine of his novel *Lorna Doone*(1869). It was probably based on the Scottish place name Lorn, the district in Argyll, and the name has therefore become very popular in Scotland.

Lorne (m)
Probably from the Scottish place name (see **Lorna**), it is used as a male name especially in Scotland and Canada.
Variant form: **Lorn**.

Lorraine (f)
From the French place name, the area in Eastern France, it has been used as a female first name since the 19th century.
Variant forms: **Loraine, Laraine, Larraine**.

Lottie, Lotty familiar forms of **Charlotte**, occasionally used as names in their own right.

Lou familiar from of **Louis** (see **Lewis**), **Louise, Louisa**.

Louella (f)
Combination of **Lou** and **Ella**.
Variant form: **Luella**; see also **Llewella, Lewella** (female forms of **Llewellyn**).

Louie familiar form of **Louis** (see **Lewis**).

Louis variant form of **Lewis**.

Louisa (f)
Female form of **Louis**, it has been used since the 18th century and became very popular at the end of the 19th. A famous bearer was Louisa M Alcott (1832-88), American author of popular stories for girls, such as *Little Women*. See also **Louise, Ouida**.
Familiar forms: **Lou, Lulu**.

Louise (f)
French female form of **Louis**, now much more popular than **Louisa**.

Familiar forms: **Lou, Lulu.**

Lovell (m)
From the surname, itself derived from Old French meaning 'little
wolf'.

Lowell (m)
From the surname, itself a variant form of **Lovell.**

Loyd variant form of **Lloyd.**

Lucas, Lúcás see **Luke.**

Lucia (f) [loo-chee-a]
Italian female form of the Latin name **Lucius,** probably from Latin
lux meaning 'light', it was the name of a 3rd-century saint, St Lucia of
Syracuse. Occasionally used in English-speaking countries. See also
Lucy, Lucilla, Lucille, Lucinda.

Lucilla (f) [loo-sil-a]
Familiar form of **Lucia,** it was the name of several early saints. Now a
name in its own right.

Lucille [looseel]
French form of **Lucilla.** Popular, especially in the USA in the mid
20th century, probably influenced by the American film actress
Lucille Ball.

Lucinda (f) [loosinda]
Familiar form of **Lucia** (though now a name in its own right), it was
the name of a character in *Don Quixote* by Cervantes (1605). It was
popular in England in the 18th century.
Familiar forms: **Cindy, Sindy** (also used as names in their own right).

Lucretia (f) [lookreesha]
Female form of the Roman family name **Lucretius,** of unknown
origin. It was the name of a Roman girl who killed herself after being
raped by the King of Rome. This legend was the subject of
Shakespeare's *The Rape of Lucrece* (the French form of the name).

Another famous bearer was Lucrezia Borgia, a member of the infamous Borgia family in medieval Italy.
The name is still used occasionally, mainly in the USA.

Lucy (f)
English form of **Lucia**, it has been in use since the Middle Ages. It was popular in the 18th and 19th centuries, less so since then, though gaining again since the 1970s. Sometimes used as an English equivalent of Irish Gaelic **Laoise**.

Ludo familiar form of **Ludovic**.

Ludovic (m)
From the Latin form, **Ludovicus**, of German **Ludwig** (see **Lewis**), it is sometimes used in the Scottish Highlands as an anglicized form of Gaelic **Maoldòmhnaich**.
Familiar form: **Ludo**.

Ludwig see **Lewis**.

Luella variant form of **Louella**.

Luke (m)
Biblical, from Greek meaning 'man from Lucania' (a district in southern Italy). In the New Testament St Luke was the author of the third Gospel and of the Acts of Apostles. He was a doctor and is regarded as the patron saint of doctors and of painters. The name has been used in English since the Middle Ages and has gained in popularity in recent decades.
Other forms: **Lucas** (Latin), **Lúcás** (Irish Gaelic).

Lulu (f)
Familiar form of German **Luisa** and also of **Louisa** and **Louise**, also used as a name in its own right.

Luther (m)
From the surname of the 16th-century German religious leader Martin Luther. The name is Germanic in origin, probably meaning 'people' + 'army'. It is popular in black American families, where it is

often given in honour of Martin Luther King (1929-68), black civil rights leader.

Lyall (m)
From the Scottish surname, itself possibly derived from an Old Norse personal name. See also **Lyle**.

Lydia (f)
From Greek meaning 'woman from Lydia' in Asia Minor. In the New Testament, Lydia, 'a seller of purple from the city of Thyatira', was converted by St Paul and entertained him at her home (Acts 16: 14-15, 40).

Lyle (m)
From the Scottish surname, itself possibly from Old French *'de l'isle'*, meaning 'of the island'. Sometimes regarded as a variant of **Lyall**.

Lyn (f)
Familiar form of names beginning or ending thus, or with this sound, such as **Linda**, **Carolyn**, also used as a name in its own right. Variant forms: **Lynn**, **Lynne**; see also **Lynette**.

Lyndon (m)
From the surname, itself from a place name, from Old English meaning 'lime tree' + 'hill'. Brought to prominence in the mid 20th century by Lyndon B Johnson, 36th president of the USA.

Lynette (f)
In some cases simply a variant of **Lyn**, but in Tennyson's *Idylls of the King* it represents an old Celtic name, possibly Welsh **Eluned**. Variant form: **Linette**.

Lynn, Lynne variant forms of **Lyn**.

Mab see **Maeve**.

Mabel (f)
Familiar form of **Amabel**, used as a name in its own right, much more frequently than the full form. Popular in the late 19th and early 20th centuries.

Maddie familiar form of **Madeleine.**

Maddison variant form of **Madison.**

Maddy familiar form of **Madeleine**

Madeleine (f)
French form of **Magdalene, Magdalen,** from Hebrew meaning
'woman from Magdala', on the Sea of Galilee, home of St Mary
Magdalen in the New Testament (Luke 8:2). The French form is now
the commonest form of the name, replacing the anglicized form
Madeline. It was formerly pronounced [maudlin], but this was
altered as the meaning 'foolishly (and drunkenly) sentimental'
developed for this word. Magdalen College, Oxford and Magdalene
College, Cambridge, however, are both still pronounced [maudlin].
Other form: **Madeline.**
Familiar forms: **Maddie, Maddy, Magda** (from German), **Alena.**

Madge familiar form of **Margaret.**

Madison (m and f)
From the surname, itself deriving from a medieval familiar form of
Magdalen. Used in the USA, probably partly in honour of James
Madison (1751-1836), fourth president. It is now used as a female as
well as a male name.
Variant form: **Maddison.**

Madonna (f)
From Italian meaning 'my lady', used as a title for the Virgin Mary,
especially in reference to Italian Renaissance paintings of the Virgin
and Child. Used as a first name in recent years by Americans of
Italian descent, and made famous by the pop star Madonna
(Ciccone).

Mae (f)
Variant of **May,** made famous in the early 20th century by Mae West,
a very plump American film actress, who gave her name to a type of
inflatable life-jacket.

Maeve (f) [mayve]
From Irish Gaelic **Meadhbh** or **Medb**, meaning 'the intoxicating one'.
It was the name of the Queen of Connacht, heroine of an Irish epic.
The name of Shakespeare's Queen **Mab** in *Romeo and Juliet* is based
on this Irish name.
Variant form: **Mave**.

Mag familiar form of **Margaret**.

Magda German familiar form of **Magdalen** (see **Madeleine**).

Magdalen, Magdalene see **Madeleine**.

Maggie (f)
Familiar form of **Margaret**, sometimes used as a name in its own
right.

Magnus (m)
From Latin meaning 'great', its use as a name originated with the
Emperor Charlemagne (in Latin Carolus Magnus). It was much used
in medieval Scandinavia, being the name of several kings of Norway.
From there it spread to Shetland and to Orkney, where the 12th-
century St Magnus gave his name to the cathedral in Kirkwall. It was
also used in Ireland, in the form **Mánas**, giving the surname Mac
Manus.

Mai Welsh form of **Mary**.

Maidie (f)
Either from a nickname, meaning 'little maid', or perhaps a familiar
form of **Margaret**.

Mair Welsh form of **Mary**.

Máire Irish Gaelic form of **Mary**.

Mairead Scottish Gaelic form of **Margaret**.

Máiréad Irish Gaelic form of **Margaret**.

Màiri Scottish Gaelic form of **Mary**.

Mairwen (f)
From Welsh meaning 'beautiful Mary'.

Maisie (f)
Familiar form of **Margaret**, or possibly of **Marjorie**, used as a name in
its own right. It was formerly popular in Scotland.

Maitland (m)
From the surname, of Norman-French origin, with doubtful meaning.

Malachi (m)[malakhy, [malaky]
Biblical, from Hebrew meaning 'my messenger'; *The Book of Malachi* is
by one of the minor prophets. It has been used in Ireland since its
adoption by a 12th-century Irish saint.
Variant form: **Malachy**.

Malcolm (m)
From Scottish Gaelic **Maol Chaluim**, meaning '(tonsured) servant of
St Columba'. It was the name of four medieval Scottish kings,
including Malcolm III, nicknamed Canmore ('Big Head') who
appears in Shakespeare's *Macbeth*, as one of the sons of King Duncan.
Now used outside Scotland, where famous bearers this century have
been the orchestral conductor Sir Malcolm Sargent and the black
American activist Malcolm X.
Other forms: **Calum** Scottish Gaelic, with variant **Callum** (both used
as names in their own right).

Mame see **Mamie**.

Mamie (f)
Familiar form of **Mary**, used as a name in its own right. It was the
name of the wife of US President Eisenhower. The form **Mame** is also
used.

Mánas Irish Gaelic form of **Magnus**.

Mandi variant form of **Mandy**

Mandy (f)
Familiar form of **Amanda**, used as a name in its own right.
Variant form: **Mandi**.

Manley (m)
From the surname, itself from a place name in Cheshire meaning
'common lands'. It was the middle name of the English poet Gerard
Manley Hopkins (1844-89).

Manny familiar form of **Emmanuel**.

Maoileas see **Miles**.

Mara (f)
Biblical from Hebrew, meaning 'bitter'. In 'The Book of Ruth' Naomi
refers to herself by this name because of her bitter experiences.

Maralyn variant form of **Marilyn**.

Marc French form of **Mark**.

Marcia (f)
Female form of Latin **Marcius**, a form of **Marcus**.
Variant form: **Marsha**.
Familiar form: **Marcie**.

Marco Italian form of **Mark**.

Marcus (m)
The original Latin form of **Mark**, it has been used in the English-
speaking world since the 19th century.

Mared Welsh form of **Margaret**.

Maree variant form of **Marie**.

Margaret (f)
From Latin **Margarita**, derived from Greek meaning 'pearl'. A 4th-
century St Margaret was martyred at Antioch. St Margaret of
Scotland was the queen of King Malcolm III in the 11th century and

she brought the name to prominence there. It was also popular in England and has remained so throughout the English-speaking world, though its frequency in this form has declined in recent years. It has been the name of queens of several countries, including England, Scotland, Denmark and France. It is also the name of Britain's first woman prime minister, Margaret Thatcher.
Other forms: **Margret, Margaretta, Margarita** (Latin, also used in Spanish and other European languages), **Marguerite** (French), **Mairead** (Scottish Gaelic [myrat]), **Máiréad** (Irish Gaelic), **Mared** (Welsh [mar-ed]); see also **Marjorie**.
Familiar forms: **Maggie, Mag, Meg, Peggy, Peggie, Peg, Madge, Marge, Margie, Margot**([margo],from **Marguerite**), **Maisie, May, Meta, Greta** (from German and Scandinavian forms), **Rita** (from Italian and Spanish forms).

Marge familiar form of **Margaret** or **Marjorie**.

Margery see **Marjorie**.

Margie familiar form of **Margaret** or **Marjorie**.

Margo variant form of **Margot**.

Margot (f) [margo]
French familiar form of **Margaret**, also used in English-speaking countries.
Other form: **Margo**.

Margret variant form of **Margaret**.

Marguerite French form of **Margaret**.

Maria (f) [ma-ree-a or ma-rye-a]
Latin form of **Mary**, also used in several European languages, including Italian, Spanish and German.

Marian (f) [marian]
Either a variant of **Marion** or thought of as a combination of **Mary + Ann**; see also **Marianne**. In the Robin Hood legends his girlfriend was known as Maid Marian.

146

Marianne (f) [marian]
French combination of **Marie** + **Anne**, also used in English-speaking countries. Marianne Faithfull is a British singer well-known in the 1960s.
Variant form: **Marianna.**

Marie (f) [maree or maree]
French form of **Mary**, used in the English-speaking world, especially in Catholic families. In Scotland it is also used as an anglicized spelling of the Gaelic form **Màiri.**
Variant form: **Maree.**

Marietta (f)
Familiar Italian-Swiss form of **Maria** or **Marie**, used as a name in its own right.

Marigold (f)
From the flower name, used occasionally since the 19th century.

Marilyn (f)
Either a familiar form of **Mary**, used as a name in its own right, or thought of as a combination of **Mary** + **Ellen**. Made popular in the mid 20th century by the film actress Marilyn Monroe.
Variant forms: **Maralyn, Marylynn.**

Marina (f)
Although long thought of as deriving from Latin meaning 'of the sea', it is more probably from the Latin family name **Marinus**, itself a derivative of **Marius**. It gained some popularity in Britain in the 1930s, when Princess Marina of Greece married the Duke of Kent (son of King George V).

Marion (f, occasionally m)
In the Middle Ages, a familiar form of French **Marie**, but now regarded as a name in its own right and often spelt **Marian**. In the Scottish Highlands it is sometimes used as an anglicized form of the Gaelic name **Mòr** or its diminutive **Mòrag.** It is also sometimes used as a male name.

Marisa (f)
A variant of **Mary**, possibly with influence from Swiss and Dutch forms.
Variant form: **Marissa**.

Marjorie (f)
The commonest modern spelling of **Margery**, originally a variant form of **Margaret**, but long used as a name in its own right. In 14th-century Scotland, Marjory Bruce was the daughter of King Robert the Bruce, who married Walter the Steward and became the founder of the Stewart dynasty.
Other forms: **Marjory, Margery, Marsali** (Scottish Gaelic).
Familiar forms: **Marge, Margie**.

Mark (m)
From Latin **Marcus**, of doubtful origin, it was the name of the author of the second Gospel, and of several other early saints. It enjoyed some popularity in the mid 20th century.
Other forms: **Marc** (French), **Marco** (Italian), both now also used in English-speaking countries.

Marlene (f) [mar-leen or mar-lay-na]
German shortening of **Maria Magdalena**, brought to prominence in the mid 20th century by the film star Marlene Dietrich (1901-92). It was also made popular by the Second World War song 'Lili Marlene'.
Variant form: **Marline**.

Marmaduke (m)
Possibly of Celtic origin, often thought to be from Irish Gaelic **Mael-Maedóc**, meaning '(tonsured) servant of Maedóc', the name of several early Irish saints. Rarely used, though formerly popular in part of Yorkshire.
Familiar form: **Duke**.

Marna see **Marnie**.

Marnie (f)
Probably a familiar form of **Marna**, a Swedish form of **Marina**. It was brought to prominence by Alfred Hitchcock's thriller film *Marnie* (1964).

Marsali Scottish Gaelic form of **Marjorie**.

Marsha variant form of **Marcia**.

Marshal variant form of **Marshall**.

Marshall (m)
From the surname, itself Norman-French of Germanic origin, meaning 'horse-servant'.
Variant form: **Marshal**.

Marta (f)
Italian form of **Martha**, also used in the English-speaking world.

Màrtainn Scottish Gaelic form of **Martin**.

Martan Irish Gaelic form of **Martin**.

Martha (f)
From Aramaic meaning 'lady'; in the New Testament (Luke 10: 38-42), Martha, the sister of Lazarus and Mary, is described as a perhaps over-careful housewife. The name has lost popularity in the 20th century. See also **Marta**.
Familiar forms: **Mattie, Marti, Marty**.

Marti familiar form of **Martin, Martha**.

Martin (m)
From Latin **Martinus**, probably from Mars, the god of war. It became popular among early Christians after the 4th-century St Martin of Tours (who on one occasion divided his coat to share it with a beggar). It was the name of several popes and also of the 16th-century German Protestant reformer, Martin Luther. A prominent 20th-century bearer of the name was Martin Luther King, the black American civil-rights campaigner.
Other forms: **Martyn, Màrtainn** (Scottish Gaelic), **Martan** (Irish Gaelic).
Familiar forms: **Marty, Marti**.

Martina (f)
Latin female form of **Martin**. Martina Navratilova is a well-known tennis-player of Czech origin.

Martiné (f) [mar-teen]
French female form of **Martin**, also used in the English-speaking world.

Marty (m and f)
Familiar form of **Martin** or of **Martha**; as a name in its own right, now usually female.

Martyn variant form of **Martin**.

Marvin variant form of **Mervyn**.

Mary (f)
Biblical, from Hebrew, a New Testament form of **Miriam**. The origin of the name is doubtful: possible connections include the sea, bitterness, rebelliousness. Though losing ground in recent decades, it is perhaps the most popular female Christian name of all time, owing to being the name of the mother of Christ. Several other New Testament women bore the name, as did numerous saints and queens through the ages. England had two reigning queens called Mary, and Scotland had the ill-fated Mary, Queen of Scots.
Other forms: **Màiri** (Scottish Gaelic [maree],and its address form **Mhàiri** [varee], sometimes anglicized as **Marie** or **Vari**), **Máire** (Irish Gaelic, sometimes anglicized as **Moya**; see also **Moira, Maura, Maureen**), **Mai** [my], **Mair**(both Welsh); see also **Maria, Marie, Marisa**.
Familiar forms: **May, Molly, Mollie, Moll, Mamie**.

Maryann (f)
Combination of **Mary** + **Ann**, popular in the 18th and 19th centuries. See also **Marian**.
Variant form: **Maryanne**.

Marylynn variant form of **Marilyn**.

Mason (m)
From the surname, itself from the occupation.

Mat familiar form of **Matthew, Matilda.**

Mathew variant form of **Matthew.**

Mathias variant form of **Matthias.**

Mathilda variant form of **Matilda.**

Matilda (f)
Norman-French of Germanic origin, meaning 'mighty' + 'battle'. This form was replaced in the Middle Ages by **Maud**, which reflected the pronunciation. But **Matilda** was used again in the 18th and 19th centuries, less commonly in the 20th. Perhaps best known from the Australian song 'Waltzing Matilda' (based on a slang phrase meaning carrying a bag around like a tramp).
Variant form: **Mathilda.**
Familiar forms: **Mattie, Mat, Tilda, Tilly, Tillie.**

Matt familiar form of **Matthew.**

Matthew (m)
Biblical, from Hebrew meaning 'gift of God'. In the New Testament it is the name of the author of the first Gospel. For long a popular name in Scotland, it enjoyed popularity in recent decades elsewhere in the English-speaking world. See also **Matthias.**
Variant form: **Mathew.**
Familiar forms: **Matt, Mattie.**

Matthias (m) [math-eye-as]
Biblical, New Testament Greek form of the Hebrew name from which **Matthew** derives. It was the name of the apostle who took the place of Judas Iscariot (Acts 1: 21-26). More popular in N America than in Britain, probably due to German influence. (In German, this form covers both names).
Variant form: **Mathias.**

Mattie familiar form of **Martha, Matilda,** and also of **Matthew.**

Maud (f)
Medieval form of **Matilda**, it was the name of the wife of William the Conqueror and of a daughter of Henry II who disputed the throne of England with her cousin Stephen. The name regained popularity in the 19th century, partly due to Tennyson's poem *Maud* (1855) and to the song from it 'Come into the garden, Maud'.
Variant form: **Maude**.
Familiar form **Maudie**, used as a name in its own right.

Maura (f)
Of Celtic origin, it was the name of an early saint; now used in Ireland as an anglicized form of Gaelic **Máire** (see **Mary**).

Maureen (f)
Anglicized form of Irish Gaelic **Máirín**, diminutive of **Máire** (see **Mary**). Now used throughout the English-speaking world. it was given prominence in the earlier 20th century by the actresses Maureen O'Sullivan and Maureen O'Hara. See also **Moreen**.
Familiar form: **Mo**.

Maurice (m)
From Latin meaning 'Moorish; dark-skinned'. It was the name of an early saint in Switzerland (hence the place name St Moritz). It was introduced into Britain by the Normans and used throughout the Middle Ages, and again from the 19th century onwards.
Variant form: **Morris**.
Familiar forms: **Mo, Morrie, Maurie**.

Mave variant form of **Maeve**, or familiar form of **Mavis**.

Mavis (f)
From an old word for a song-thrush (still used in Scotland, though the name is not specially popular there). Its use began in England in the late 19th century, probably owing to a character of this name in Marie Corelli's novel *The Sorrows of Satan* (1895).
Familiar form: **Mave**.

Max familiar form of **Maximilian** or **Maxwell**, also used as a name in its own right.

Maxie familiar form of **Max** or of **Maxine**, also used as a female name in its own right.

Maximilian (m)
Based on Latin *maximus*, meaning 'greatest', it was the name of 3rd-century saint, and later became a favourite name in the family of the Hapsburg emperors. Never popular in Britain, except in the familiar form.
Familiar form: **Max**.

Maxine (f)
20th-century female form of **Max**.
Familiar form: **Maxie**, also used as a name in its own right.

Maxwell (m)
From the Scottish surname, itself from a place name, probably meaning 'Magnus's well'. It is now used as a first name throughout the English-speaking world.
Familiar forms: **Max, Maxie**.

May (f)
Familiar form of **Mary** or **Margaret**, also used as a name in its own right, often by association with the name of the the fifth month. Like **April** and **June**, it enjoyed popularity thus in the early 20th century.
See also **Maya**.
Variant form: **Mae**.

Maya (f) [my-a]
A variant form of **May**, though the American writer Maya Angelou (1929-) was so called in childhood because her brother referred to her as 'mya sista'.

Maynard (m)
From the surname, itself Norman-French of Germanic origin, meaning 'strength' + 'hardy'. A famous bearer was the economist John Maynard Keynes (1883-1946).

Meadhbh see **Maeve**.

Meaghan, Meagan variant forms of **Megan**.

Medb see **Maeve**.

Meg familiar form of **Margaret**.

Megan (f) [meggan]
Welsh form of **Meg**. Megan Lloyd-George was the daughter of the
early 20th-century British prime minister David Lloyd-George.
Variant forms: **Meghan, Meaghan, Meagan** (used in N America and
Australia, in the mistaken belief that the name is of Irish origin).
Meic familiar form of **Meical**.

Meical Welsh form of **Michael**.
Familiar form: **Meic**.

Meilyr (m) [may-ler]
From Welsh meaning 'chief' + 'ruler'.

Meinwen (f) [main-wen]
From Welsh meaning 'white, fair, holy'.

Meirion (m) [merry-on]
From Welsh, ultimately from the Latin for **Mary**.

Mel familiar form of **Melville, Melvin**, also used as a name in its
own right. As a female name, it is a familiar form of **Melanie** or other
names beginning thus.

Melanie (f) [melany]
French form of Latin **Melania**, from Greek meaning 'black, dark', it
was the name of two early Roman saints. It was popular in the
Middle Ages and again in the 20th century.
Variant forms: **Melany, Melony**.
Familiar form: **Mel**.

Melinda (f)
A combination of mel- as in names such as **Melanie** and **Melissa**,
with the ending -inda, as in **Belinda**.

Melissa (f)
From Greek meaning 'bee'. It was known in earlier centuries, but has become very popular in recent decades, especally in N America.
Familiar form: **Lissa.**

Melody (f)
From the word meaning 'tune', it has gained some popularity from the mid 20th century.

Melony variant form of **Melanie.**

Melville (m)
From the Scottish surname, itself of Norman-French origin, based on a northern French place name. It is now used as a first name throughout the English-speaking world.
Familiar form: **Mel.**

Melvin (m)
Probably from the Scottish surname, itself a variant of **Melville.**
Variant form: **Melvyn.** Melvyn Bragg is a writer and television presenter.
Familiar form: **Mel.**

Menna (f)
Of uncertain origin. Popular in Wales, possibly because parents connect it with place names such as Menai.

Mercia (f)
From the name of an Anglo-Saxon kingdom in the English Midlands, it is popular in Wales and in the bordering areas of England.

Mercy (f)
From the virtue, as so many other such names, introduced by the Puritans in the 17th century.
Familiar form: **Merry** (which was the name of one of the Pecksniff daughters in Dickens' *Martin Chuzzlewit*).

Meredith (m and f)
From Old Welsh, probably meaning 'great lord'. Formerly a male name, it has also been used in recent years as a female one.

Variant form: Meridith.
Familiar form: **Merry** (f).

Merfyn see **Mervyn.**

Meridith variant form of **Meredith.**

Meriel variant form of **Muriel.**

Merle(f and m)
May be a variant of **Meriel**, or more probably from the French word
for 'blackbird'. Merle Oberon was a film actress of the mid 20th
century. Mainly a female name, it is also used for males, especially in
N America.

Merlin (m and f)
Anglicized form of Welsh **Myrddin**, probably meaning 'sea' + 'hill,
fort', it was the name of the magician in the legends of King Arthur.
Used in the 20th century, at first only as a male and later also as a
female name.
Variant form: **Merlyn** (female).

Merrill (f)
Either a variant form of **Muriel**, or from the surname, which is in any
case derived from it. Popular in the USA.

Merry familiar form of **Meredith** (as a female name) or of **Mercy**.

Merton (m)
From the surname, itself from various place names meaning 'lake' +
'settlement'.

Merv familiar form of **Mervyn.**

Mervin variant form of **Mervyn.**

Mervyn (m)
Anglicized form of Welsh **Merfyn**, probably meaning 'marrow' +
'eminent'. It is commonly used in Jewish families.
Variant forms: **Mervin, Marvin.**

Familiar form: **Merv**.

Meryl variant form of **Muriel**, brought to prominence in the 1980s by the American actress Meryl Streep.

Meta familiar form of **Margaret**.

Mhàiri Scottish Gaelic, see **Mary**.

Mia (f) [mee-a]
Either a Scandinavian familiar form of **Maria**, or Italian and Spanish for 'my'. It has been brought to prominence in the late 20th century by the American film actress Mia Farrow.

Michael (m)
Biblical, from Hebrew (via Greek) meaning 'Who is like the Lord?' It was the name of one of the archangels; regarded as the guardian angel of Israel and as the patron saint of soldiers, he is often depicted with a sword. The name was at one time very popular in Ireland, so that the familiar form **Mick** came to be used to refer to an Irishman. See also **Mitchell**.
Other forms: **Mícheál** (Irish Gaelic [mee-howl]), **Mìcheil** (Scottish Gaelic [mee-khil]), **Meical**, **Meic** (both Welsh).
Familiar forms: **Mike**, **Mick**, **Micky**, all used as names in their own right.

Michaela (f)
Female form of **Michael**.
Variant form: **Mikaela**.

Mícheál Irish Gaelic form of **Michael**.

Mìcheil Scottish Gaelic form of **Michael**.

Michèle (f)
Female form of **Michel**, French form of **Michael**, widely used in the English-speaking world.
Variant form: **Michelle**.

Mick familiar form of **Michael**.

Micky familiar form of **Michael**.

Mikaela variant form of **Michaela**.

Mike familiar form of **Michael**.

Mildred (f)
From Old English meaning 'gentle' + 'strength', it was the name of a
7th-century English saint. Not used in the Middle Ages but revived
later. It became popular in the early 20th century, especially in N
America.
Familiar forms: **Millie, Milly**.

Miles (m)
Norman-French of doubtful origin. May be connected with Latin
miles meaning 'soldier' or may be a variant of **Michael**. In Ireland it
has been used, especially in the form **Myles**, as an anglicized form of
Gaelic names such as **Maoileas** [mao-lus], meaning '(tonsured)
servant of Jesus'. Miles Davis is a well-known jazz trumpeter.
Variant form: **Myles**.

Millicent (f)
Norman-French of Germanic origin, meaning 'work' + 'strength'.
Popular in Britain in the late 19th and early 20th centuries.
Familiar forms: **Millie, Milly**.

Millie familiar form of **Mildred, Millicent** or **Camilla**.

Milly familiar form of **Mildred, Millicent** or **Camilla**.

Milton (m)
From the surname, itself from numerous place names deriving from
Old English meaning 'mill' + 'settlement'.

Mima (f)
Familiar form of **Jemima**, occasionally used as a name in its own
right.

Mimi (f) [meemee]
Italian familiar form of **Maria**, it was the name of the heroine of
Puccini's opera *La Bohème*. Used occasionally in the English-speaking
world since then.

Mina (f)
Familiar form of **Wilhelmina, Williamina,** formerly popular in
Scotland.

Minnie (f)
Probably a familiar form of **Wilhelmina**, popular in Britain in the late
19th and early 20th centuries.

Mirabelle (f)
French, from Latin meaning 'to be admired'. In this and in the Italian
form **Mirabella** it was used in the Middle Ages. the form **Mirabel**
was used as a male name in the 17th and 18th centuries.

Miranda (f)
From Latin meaning 'to be admired', it was invented by Shakespeare
as the name of the heroine in *The Tempest* (1611).

Miriam (f)
Biblical, from the Hebrew name of which **Mary** is a later form. In the
Old Testament Miriam was the sister of Moses and Aaron (Exodus
15: 20-21). The name is still popular in Jewish families. Miriam
Makeba is a well-known African singer.
Variant form: **Myriam.**

Mitch familiar form of **Mitchell.**

Mitchell (m)
From the surname, itself from a medieval form of **Michael.**
Familiar form: **Mitch.** Mitch Mitchell is a well-known rock drummer.

Mitzi (f)
German familiar form of **Maria.** Brought to prominence by the
American film actress Mitzi Gaynor (born Francesca Mitzi von
Gerber). Mitzi Cunliffe is an American sculptor.

Mo familiar form of **Maurice** or **Maureen**.

Moira (f)
Anglicized form of **Máire**, Irish Gaelic form of **Mary**. It is used throughout the English-speaking world, and has been especially popular in Scotland.
Variant form: **Moyra**.

Móirín see **Mór**.

Moll, Mollie, Molly familiar forms of **Mary**.

Mona (f)
Anglicized form of Irish Gaelic **Muadhnait**,the name of an early Irish saint, meaning 'noble'. It is also the Latin name for the Isle of Man and for the island of Anglesey, and some parents may have connected the name with those.

Monica (f)
Of doubtful origin; Greek *monos* meaning 'alone' and Latin *monere* meaning 'to warn, advise' have been suggested. The 4th-century St Monica was the mother of St Augustine and had a powerful influence on his life.
Other form: **Monique** (French [moneek]).

Monroe (m)
From the Scottish surname, more commonly spelt **Munro**, itself of doubtful origin, probably from a place name. As a first name it has been more popular in the USA than in Britain, possibly influenced by James Monroe (1758-1831), fifth president of the USA.
Variant forms: **Monro, Munro, Munroe**.

Montague (m)
From the surname, itself based on a Norman-French place name meaning 'pointed hill'.
Variant form: **Montagu**.
Familiar form: **Monty**.

Montgomery (m)
From the surname, of Norman-French origin, from a place name in

Normandy. Not common as a first name, it may have been given
some prominence by the World War II Field-Marshal Montgomery,
often known by the familiar form **Monty.**

Monty familiar form of **Montague, Montgomery.**

Mór (f)
Scottish and Irish Gaelic meaning 'great' formerly a very common
name in Ireland and in the Scottish Highlands. It has familiar forms,
used as names in their own right, in Scottish Gaelic **Mòrag,** and in
Irish **Móirín,** anglicized as **Moreen.**

Morag (f)
From Scottish Gaelic **Mòrag,** familiar form of **Mòr,** meaning 'great',
now used as a name in its own right throughout Scotland and to a
lesser extent in other parts of the English-speaking world. Sometimes
anglicized as **Marion** or formerly, and mysteriously, as **Sarah.**

Moray variant form of **Murray.**

Mordecai (m)
Biblical, of uncertain origin. In the Old Testament Mordecai was the
cousin and foster-father of Esther (Esther 2:5-7). The name was
popular with Puritans in the 17th century; it is now mainly used in
Jewish families.

Moreen (f)
From Irish Gaelic **Móirín,** familiar form of **Mór;** also confused with
Maureen.

Morgan (m and f)
Common Welsh surname and male first name, of doubtful origin.
Also used occasionally, elsewhere, as a female name, possibly with
reference to Morgan le Fay, the sorceress half-sister of King Arthur in
Arthurian legend; see also **Fay.**

Morley (m)
From the surname, itself from Old English meaning 'wood' +
'clearing'.

Morna variant of **Myrna**, used especially in Scotland.

Morrie familiar form of **Maurice**.

Morris variant form of **Maurice**.

Mort familiar form of **Mortimer, Morton**.

Mortie familiar form of **Mortimer**.

Mortimer (m)
From the surname, itself of Norman-French origin, from a place name meaning 'dead'+ 'sea'. It has been used as a first name since the 19th century. A famous bearer was the archaeologist Sir Mortimer Wheeler (1890-1976).
Familiar forms: **Mort, Mortie, Morty**.

Morton (m)
From the surname, itself from several place names, from Old English meaning 'moor' + 'settlement'. It is also used as a Jewish first name, as a substitute for **Moses**.
Familiar form: **Mort**.

Morty familiar form of **Mortimer**.

Morven (f)
From several Scottish place names, either the district of Morvern in Argyll, from Gaelic possibly meaning 'sea-gap', or from mountains called Morven in Caithness and Aberdeenshire, from Gaelic meaning 'big mountain'.

Morwenna (f) [mor-wen-na]
From a Welsh word meaning 'maiden', it was the name of a 5th-century Cornish saint. Used in the 20th century in Cornwall and Wales.

Moses (m)
Biblical, of obsure origin, it was the name of the Old Testament law-giver who freed the Israelites from Egypt. Popular with Puritans in the 17th century, and still used in Jewish families, though now

usually in the Hebrew form **Moshe** [mo-shay] or **Moishe** [moy-shay].

Mostyn (m)
From the Welsh surname, itself from a place name, derived from Old
English meaning 'moss' + 'settlement'.

Moya see **Mary**.

Moyra variant form of **Moira**.

Muireall, Muirgheal see **Muriel**.

Mungo (m)
From Scottish Gaelic, of obscure origin, it was the nickname, by
which the the 6th-century St Kentigern, the patron saint of Glasgow,
was generally known. Used occasionally in Scotland. A famous
bearer was Mungo Park (1771-1806), Scottish explorer in Africa.

Munro, Munroe variant forms of **Monroe**.

Murdo (m)
From Scottish Gaelic **Murchadh**, probably meaning 'sea-warrior'; the
Gaelic form is also found in Ireland. Very common in the Highlands
of Scotland.
Variant form: **Murdoch** (commoner as a surname, though
occasionally found as a first name in the Scottish Lowlands).

Muriel (f)
Possibly from Irish Gaelic **Muirgheal** meaning 'sea' + 'bright',
though there are similar forms in Breton and Welsh, which may also
have provided origins. It had some popularity in the late 19th and
early 20th centuries, especially in Scotland; a well-known bearer is
the Scottish novelist Muriel Spark. See also **Merrill, Meryl**.
Other forms: **Meriel, Muireall** (Scottish Gaelic).

Murray (m)
From the Scottish surname, itself from the place name Moray, the
area in north-east Scotland. The name is now also used outside

Scotland, especially in Canada. Murray Walker is a well-known English sports commentator.
Variant form: **Moray.**

Myf familiar form of **Myfanwy.**

Myfanwy (f) [mi-van-wee]
From Welsh meaning 'my dear woman', it has been used in Wales since the late 19th century.
Familiar form: **Myf** [miv].

Myles variant form of **Miles.**

Myra (f)
Invented by a 17th-century English poet and used only in literature until the early 19th century. Since then it has been in general use, especially in Scotland. Though its origin is unknown, various theories have been put forward: that it is a variant of **Mary**, or that it comes from the Latin for 'myrrh' or meaning 'to admire'.

Myriam variant form of **Miriam.**

Myrna(f)
From Irish Gaelic **Muirne** meaning 'beloved' or 'high-spirited, festive', it was the name of the mother of the legendary hero Fionn Mac Cumhaill (Finn Mac Cool) It has been used outside Ireland, given some prominence in the mid 20th century by the film actress Myrna Loy.
Variant form: **Morna.**

Myrrdin see **Merlin.**

Myrtle (f)
From the plant name, used, like so many others, as a female name since the late 19th century.

Nadezhda see **Nadia.**

Nadia (f)
Familiar form of the Russian name **Nadezhda**, meaning 'hope',

occasionally used as a name in its own right in English-speaking countries, where a well-known bearer is the ballerina Nadia Nerina. It is also used in France, as in the name of the musician Nadia Boulanger (1887-1979).
Other forms: **Nadya**, **Nadine** (French [na-deen], but also used in English-speaking countries).

Nan familiar form of **Ann, Nancy**.

Nana (f)
Familiar form of **Anna** or **Hannah**. Less used as a name now as it is used by many children as a name for their grandmother.

Nance familiar form of **Nancy**.

Nancy (f)
Probably originally a familiar form of **Ann**, but frequently used as a name in its own right. Less popular in recent decades, perhaps partly owing to the use of the word 'nancy-boy' to refer to a homosexual or effeminate man.
Familiar forms: **Nance. Nan.**

Nanette (f)
Familiar form of **Nan** (and thus of **Ann**), used as a name in its own right. It was brought to prominence in the 1920s by the musical comedy and film *No, No, Nanette*. A well-known bearer is the actress Nanette Newman.
Variant form: **Nannette**.

Nanny, Nannie familiar Scottish forms of **Ann**.

Naomi (f) [nay-o-mee]
Biblical from Hebrew, meaning 'pleasantness'. In the Old Testament, in *The Book of Ruth*, Naomi was the mother-in-law of Ruth, with whom she stayed after the death of her husband. The name is popular in Jewish families.

Nat familiar form of **Nathan, Nathaniel**, or of **Natalia, Natalie**.

Natalia (f)
Russian from Latin, meaning 'birthday (of Christ)', i.e. Christmas.
Used occasionally in Britain for girls born on 25 December. See also
Natalie, Natasha.
Variant form: **Natalya.**
Familiar forms: **Nattie, Nat.**

Natalie (f)
French form of **Natalia**, it has been more widely used in Britain than
the Russian form. Given some prominence in the mid 20th century by
the actress Natalie Wood. See also **Natasha.**
Variant form **Nathalie.**
Familiar form: **Nattie, Nat.**

Natalya variant form of **Natalia.**

Natasha (f)
Russian familiar form of **Natalia**, used in English-speaking countries
in recent decades. It was the name of the heroine of Tolstoy's *War and
Peace.*
Familiar form: **Tasha.**

Nathalie variant form of **Natalie.**

Nathan (m)[nay-than]
Biblical, from Hebrew meaning 'he (i.e. God) has given', it was the
name of an Old Testament prophet (2 Samuel 7 and 12). Commonly
used in Jewish families.
Familiar form: **Nat.**

Nathanael variant form of **Nathaniel.**

Nathaniel (m)
Biblical from Hebrew meaning 'God has given', in the New
Testament it was the name of one of the followers of Christ (John
1:45, 21:2). It is more popular in N America than in Britain, especially
in black families. Nathaniel Hawthorne was a 19th-century American
writer.
Variant form: **Nathanael.**
Familiar form: **Nat.**

Nattie familiar form of **Natalia, Natalie.**

Neal, Neale variant forms of **Neil.**

Ned, Neddy, Neddie familiar forms of **Edward** (and of other names beginning with Ed-).

Neil (m)
Anglicized form of Gaelic **Niall**, probably meaning 'champion' though the origin is disputed. Long popular in Ireland and in Scotland, especially in the Highlands, it has now spread to other parts of the English-speaking world. Neil Armstrong, the American astronaut, was one of the first two men to land on the moon in 1969. See also **Nigel.**
Other forms: **Neal, Neale, Niel, Neill, Nial, Niall** (Scottish Gaelic).
Familiar form: **Neilie** (Scottish).

Nell (f)
Familiar form of **Helen, Ellen,** or **Eleanor,** also used as a name in its own right. Nell Gwyn, mistress of King Charles II, was Eleanor, and Little Nell in Dickens' *Great Expectations* was Elinor.

Nellie, Nelly (f)
Familiar forms of **Helen, Ellen, Eleanor** or of **Nell.** Dame Nellie Melba (1861-1931) was the stage name of a famous Australian opera singer.

Nelson (m)
From the surname, meaning 'son of Neil', or 'son of Nell', it probably became used as a first name because of the fame of Admiral Lord Nelson (1758-1805), victor of the Battle of Trafalgar. It is most commonly used in N America, but at the present time it is best known as the name of the South African President Nelson Mandela.

Nena variant form of **Nina.**

Nerys (f) [nare-is]
The feminine form of a Welsh word meaning 'lord', it is gaining popularity in Wales.

167

Nessa familiar form of **Vanessa** or **Agnes**.

Nessie, Nessy familiar forms of **Agnes**, formerly popular in Scotland, but now less so, perhaps partly because the name is used as a nickname for the mysterious Loch Ness Monster.

Nesta (f)
Welsh familiar form of **Agnes**.

Netta familiar form of **Henrietta, Annette, Janet**, or of other names with similar endings.

Nettie, Netty familiar forms of **Annette, Janet**, or of other names with similar endings.

Nev familiar form of **Neville**.

Nevil, Nevile, Nevill variant forms of **Neville**.

Neville (m)
From the surname, Norman-French in origin, derived from French meaning 'new town'. It has been used as a first name since the 19th century and famous bearers include the British Prime Minister, Neville Chamberlain and the novelist Nevil Shute.
Variant forms: **Nevil, Nevile, Nevill**.
Familiar form: **Nev**.

Newt familiar form of **Newton**.

Newton (m)
From the surname, from the widespread English place name, meaning 'new' + 'settlement'. More popular in N America.
Familiar form: **Newt** (brought to prominence in the 1990s by the American politician Newt Gingrich).

Ngaio (f) [nye-o]
A New Zealand name, from Maori meaning 'clever'. Known in Britain as the name of the New Zealand novelist Dame Ngaio Marsh (1899-82).

Ngaire (f) [nye-ree]
New Zealand name of Maori origin, of obscure meaning.
Variant form: **Nyree** (anglicized).

Nia (f)
Welsh form of **Niamh**.

Nial, Niall see **Neil**.

Niamh (f) [nee-av]
From Irish Gaelic meaning 'brightness'. In Irish legend Niamh was
the name of the supernatural lover of Oisín (Ossian), son of Fionn
Mac Cumhaill (Finn Mac Cool).

Nichol variant form of **Nicol**.

Nichola variant form of **Nicola**.

Nicholas (m)
From Greek meaning 'victory' + 'people'. The 4th-century St Nicholas
was the patron saint of children and of sailors, as well as of Greece
and Russia. In his guise as bringer of Christmas presents he is known
as Santa Claus, based on a Dutch form of his name. See also **Nicol**.
Variant forms: **Nicolas, Nickolas**.
Familiar forms: **Nick, Nicky, Nickie, Nik, Niki, Nikki, Nico**.

Nichole variant form of **Nicole**.

Nick familiar form of **Nicholas**.

Nicki familiar form of **Nicola** or **Nicole**.

Nickie familiar form of **Nicholas** or of **Nicola, Nicole**.

Nickolas variant form of **Nicholas**.

Nicky familiar form of **Nicholas**, or of **Nicola, Nicole**.

Nico familiar form of **Nicholas**, or of **Nicola, Nicole**.

Nicol (m)
Medieval form of **Nicholas**, long used in Scotland and now gaining popularity elsewhere. It was the name of a character in Sir Walter Scott's *Rob Roy*, Bailie Nicol Jarvie.
Variant form: **Nichol, Nicoll.**

Nicola (f)
Female form of **Nicholas**; see also **Nicole.**
Variant form: **Nichola.**
Familiar forms: **Nickie, Nicky, Nicki, Niki, Nikki, Nico.**

Nicolas variant form of **Nicholas.**

Nicole (f) [neekol]
French female form of **Nicholas**, now used throughout the English-speaking world; see also **Nicola.**
Variant form: **Nichole.**
Familiar forms: **Nickie, Nicky, Nicki, Nikki, Nico**; see also **Nicolette.**

Nicolette (f)
French familiar form of **Nicole**, used occasionally in the English-speaking world; the familiar form **Colette** is probably more widely used as a name in its own right.

Nicoll variant form of **Nicol.**

Niel variant form of **Neil.**

Nigel (m)
From **Nigellus**, a medieval Latin form of an early Gaelic form of **Neil**. It was sometimes thought to be derived from Latin *niger*, meaning 'black'. It became popular in Scotland in the 19th century, after use by writers such as Sir Walter Scott, one of whose novels is entitled *The Fortunes of Nigel* (1822). In recent decades it has gained popularity in other parts of the English-speaking world. Nigel Mansell is a world-famous racing driver.

Nik familiar form of **Nicholas.**

Niki, Nikki familiar forms of **Nicola, Nicole** or occasionally of **Nicholas**.

Nina (f) [neena]
Originally a familiar form of Russian names such as **Antonina**; now used as a name in its own right.
Variant form: **Nena**.

Ninian (m)
Of Celtic origin with doubtful meaning, it was the name of a 5th-century saint who brought Christianity to southern Scotland. The name is still used in Scotland.

Nita (f)
Familiar form of Spanish names such as **Juanita**, used as a name in its own right in the English-speaking world.

Noah (m)
Biblical from Hebrew, of doubtful meaning, but possibly meaning 'rest' or 'comfort'. In the Old Testament, it was the name of the builder of the Ark which saved his family when God sent a flood to destroy mankind (Genesis 5-9). A famous bearer of the name was Noah Webster (1758-1843), American dictionary-maker whose name has become a byword for dictionaries in the USA.

Noalene variant form of **Nolene**.

Noam (m) [nome]
From Hebrew meaning 'pleasantness' (as the female name **Naomi**), it is used in American Jewish families. The most famous bearer is the American linguist (Avril) Noam Chomsky (1928-).

Noel (m) [no-el]
From French meaning 'Christmas'; the name was originally used for both sexes, but is now almost always male in this form. A well-known bearer in the 20th century was the English playwright and composer Noel Coward (1899-1973).
Other forms: **Noël, Nowell** (rare, and perhaps influenced by the use of this form in Christmas carols).

Noele (f) [no-ell]
Female form of **Noel**; see also **Noelene**.
Variant form: **Noelle**.

Noeleen variant form of **Noelene**.

Noelene (f)
Female form of **Noel**, popular in Australia; see also **Noele**, **Nolene**.
Variant form: **Noeleen**.

Nola (f)
Familiar form of **Fionnuala**, or sometimes regarded as a female form
of **Nolan**.

Nolan (m)
From the Irish surname **Ó Nualláin**, itself from a first name, probably
meaning 'noble, famous'.

Noleen variant form of **Nolene**.

Nolene (f)
Female form of **Nolan**, or variant of **Noelene**. It is popular in
Australia.
Variant forms: **Noleen**, **Noalene**.

Noll, Nollie familiar forms of **Oliver**.

Nona (f)
From Latin meaning 'ninth', it was formerly sometimes used for the
ninth child (or ninth daughter of a family); uncommon in recent
times, as is a ninth child.

Nora (f)
Originally a familiar form of names such as **Honora**, **Leonora**,
Eleanor, it has long been used as a name in its own right. Often
considered to be Irish.
Other forms: **Norah**, **Nóra** (Irish Gaelic).

Norbert (m)
Of Germanic origin, meaning 'north' + 'bright, famous', it was used

in the Middle Ages and then again from the 19th century on, more frequently in N America than in Britain.
Familiar forms: **Norrie, Bert, Bertie.**

Noreen (f)
Irish familiar form of **Nora,** used as a name in its own right.
Variant forms: **Norene, Norine.**

Norm familiar form of **Norman.**

Norma (f)
In Latin means 'a rule', though this may not have influenced the name, which began with Bellini's opera *Norma* (1932). It has also been used, especially in the Scottish Highlands, as a female version of **Norman.**

Norman (m)
From Germanic meaning 'north' + 'man', i.e. Norseman, Scandinavian. It was used in the Middle Ages (both before and after the Norman Conquest of England) and again from the 19th century on. It has long been popular in Scotland, especially in the Highlands where it is used as an anglicized version of the Gaelic name **Tormod,** itself of Norse origin, meaning 'Thor (the Norse god of war)' + 'wrath'. It has been particularly favoured in the Macleod clan as it was the name of one of its progenitors.
Familiar forms: **Norrie, Norm.**

Nornie familiar form of **Leonora.**

Norrie familiar form of **Norman** or **Norbert.**

Norris (m)
From the surname, itself of Norman-French origin, from Old French meaning 'northener'.

Norton (m)
From the surname, itself derived from numerous place names, from Old English meaning 'north' + 'settlement'.

Nowell variant form of **Noel.**

Nuala (f)
Familiar form of **Fionnuala**, also used as a name in its own right.

Nye (m)
Familiar form of **Aneurin**, well known in the mid 20th century as the name by which the politician Aneurin Bevan (1897-1960) was normally known.

Nyree (f)
Variant form of the Maori name **Ngaire**, given some prominence in Britain by the actress Nyree Dawn Porter.

Obadiah (m)
Biblical, from Hebrew meaning 'God's servant'. In the Old Testament, Obadiah , a minor prophet, gave his name to one of the books of the Bible. The name has only been used occasionally since the 19th century.

Oberon other form of **Auberon.**

Ocean (m and f)
From the word 'ocean' used as a name for children born at sea.

Octavia (f)
From the feminine form of the Latin word meaning 'eighth'. Octavia Hill was the 19th-century founder of the National Trust.

Octavius (m)
From the Roman family name **Octavius,** itself from Latin meaning 'eighth'.

Odell (m)
From the surname, itself from a place name meaning 'hill of woad'

Odella (f)
Female form of **Odell**.

Odelyn (f)
Female form of **Odell**.

Odette (f)
French female form of a Germanic name meaning 'riches'. It has been used occasionally in Britain in the 20th century, especially after World War II, in honour of the war heroine Odette Churchill.

Odhrán see Oran.

Odile (f)
French female form of a Germanic name meaning 'riches', but considered in the USA to be a female form of **Odell**.

Odo variant form of Otto.

Ogden (m)
From the surname, itself from a place name meaning 'valley of oak'. Uncommon as a first name, it was made famous by the 20th-century writer of humorous verse, Ogden Nash.

Oighrig see Henrietta, Euphemia.

Oisín see Ossian.

Olave (m)
From Old Norse meaning 'ancestor'.
Other form: **Aulay** (Scottish, from Gaelic form **Amhlaigh**).

Olga (f)
The Russian form of Scandinavian **Helga** meaning 'holy'.

Olive (f)
From Latin meaning 'olive tree', it was one of the many names derived from plant names introduced in the 19th century.

Oliver (m)
From the French name Olivier, probably from Latin meaning 'olive tree'. Famous bearers of the name include Oliver Cromwell (1599-1658), the poet Oliver Goldsmith (1728-74) and St Oliver Plunket (1629-81).
Familiar forms: **Ollie, Noll, Nollie.**

Olivia (f)
Originally the Italian form of **Olive** but long considered as a name in
its own right with romantic and aristocratic associations. Olivia is one
of the heroines in Shakespeare's *Twelfth Night* and in Goldsmith's
The Vicar of Wakefield (1766). Olivia Newton-John is an Australian
actress-singer.
Familiar form: **Livy.**

Ollie familiar form of **Oliver**

Olwen (f)
From Welsh meaning 'white footprint' from the legend of beautiful
Olwen who left tracks of white flowers wherever she trod.
Variant forms: **Olwyn, Olwin.**

Omar (m)
Biblical, from Hebrew meaning 'eloquent'. (Genesis 36:11). Two
influential examples are the Persian poet Omar Khayyam, whose
translated poems were very popular from the 1930s onwards and
Omar Sharif, 20th-century film star.

Omega (f)
From the last letter of the Greek alphabet, used occasionally for the
last-born child.

Ona (f)
Variant form of **Una**, but sometimes also a familiar form of names
ending in 'ona' such as **Ilona.**

Onóra Irish Gaelic form of **Honora.**

Oona variant form of **Una.**

Oonagh variant form of **Una.**

Oonie familiar form of **Una.**

Opal (f)
The name of the jewel, itself from Sanskrit meaning 'precious stone'.

Ophelia (f)
From Greek meaning 'help'. Ophelia in Shakespeare's *Hamlet* kills herself for love of Hamlet.

Ophrah variant form of **Orpah.**

Oprah variant form of **Orpah.**

Ora (f)
Of uncertain origin, but possibly a familiar form of **Dora** and **Cora** or from Latin meaning 'pray'.

Oran (m)
From Irish Gaelic **Odhrán** probably meaning 'green' or 'sallow'. One of St Columba's disciples bore this name.

Orfa variant form of **Orpah.**

Oria (f) see **Órla.**

Oriana (f)
From Latin meaning 'sunrise'. Popular in 16th-century literature and a name given by poets to Queen Elizabeth I.

Oriel (f)
Considerd by some to be from Latin meaning 'porch', but by others to come from Germanic meaning 'battle heat'. Earliest records show the spelling as **Auriel** , but it is impossible to tell which was the original.
Other form: **Oriole.**

Oriole variant form of **Oriel.**

Órla (f)
From Irish Gaelic meaning 'golden princess'.
Other forms: **Órlaidh, Oria, Orlagh** (last two anglicized).

Orlagh see **Órla**

Órlaidh see **Órla**

Orlando (m)
Italian form of **Roland**, occasionally used in the English speaking world. [It is the name of the main character in Virginia Woolf's novel *Orlando*.]

Ormerod (m)
From the surname, itself meaning 'Orm's place'.

Ormonde (m)
From the Irish surname, itself from Irish Gaelic meaning 'red' or from the place name, itself meaning 'East Munster'.

Orpah (f)
Biblical, from Hebrew of uncertain meaning. In the Old Testament, the name appears in the Book of Ruth (1:44).
Variant forms: **Orpra, Oprah Orpha, Ophrah, Orphy, Orfa**. Oprah Winfrey, television star, has made the name a household word.

Orson (m)
From Norman-French meaning 'little bear'. According to a 15th-century tale, Orson was a child seized by bears and brought up in the forest as a bear cub. Orson Welles, the writer and actor, was a famous 20th-century bearer of the name.

Ortho (m)
From Greek meaning 'straight', sometimes used in Cornwall.

Orval variant form of **Orville**.

Orville (m)
Invented by Fanny Burney for the hero of her novel *Evelina* (1778). A famous bearer was Orville Wright (1871-1848), pioneer of flying.
Variant form: **Orval**.

Osbert (m)
From Old English meaning 'god' + 'bright'. The writer Osbert Sitwell was a rare 20th- century example.
Familiar forms: **Oz, Ozzie**.

Osborne (m)
From Old English meaning 'god' + 'bear'. It is now usually a surname, except in black American families.

Oscar (m)
From form Irish Gaelic, possibly meaning 'dear' + 'love'. Oscar Wilde, dramatist (1854-1900) was a famous example.

Osmond (m)
From two Old English words meaning 'god' + 'protector'.
Variant form: **Osmund.**

Ossian (m)
From Irish Gaelic **Oisín [o-sheen]**, meaning 'little deer'. In Irish legend it was the name of the son of Finn mac Cumhaill (Finn Mac Cool). It was brought to prominence in the 18th century by the Scot James MacPherson, with his controversial poems, claimed to derive from legendary times.

Oswald (m)
From Old English meaning 'god' + 'power'. St Oswald was a 7th-century saint and King of Northumbria.
Familiar forms: **Oz, Ozzie.**

Oswin (m)
From Old English meaning 'god' + 'friend'. Rare in the 20th century.

Osyth (f)
The name of a 7th-century saint, rare in the 20th century.

Otho variant form of **Otto.**

Otis (m)
The surname used as a first name, itself derived from **Otto**. Otis Reading was a famous soul singer of the mid-20th century.

Otilie variant form of **Ottilie.**

Ottilie (f)
French and German female version of **Otto**.
Variant form: **Otilie**.

Otto (m)
From Germanic meaning 'possessions'. A German name used freely
in the English-speaking world until the two World Wars.
Variant forms: **Odo** and **Otho**.

Ottoline (f)
Originally a diminutive female version of **Otto**. It was made famous
as a name in its own right by Lady Ottoline Morrell (1873-1938)
famous for her literary connections in London.

Ouida (f)
From baby pronunciation of **Louisa**. Writer Marie Louise de la
Ramée (1839-1908) used it as a pseudonym.

Owain Welsh form of **Owen**.

Owen (m)
From a Welsh translation of the Latin meaning 'well-born'. A name
respected in Wales because of the 14th-century hero Owen
Glendower.
Other form: **Owain** (Welsh).

Oz familiar form of **Osbert, Oswald**.

Ozzie familiar form of **Osbert, Oswald**.

Paddy familiar form of **Patrick**.

Pádraig see **Patrick**.

Page variant form of **Paige**.

Paget variant form of **Paige**.

Paige (f)
From the surname meaning 'attendant' or 'page'.

Variant forms **Page, Paget.**

Paloma (f)
From Spanish meaning 'dove'. It is the name of the daughter of the painter Pablo Picasso.

Pam familiar form of **Pamela.**

Pamala variant form of **Pamela.**

Pamela (f)
Possibly from Greek meaning 'honeyed sweetness'. Invented by the poet Sir Philip Sidney in the 16th century and used by Samuel Richardson for the virtuous heroine of his novel *Pamela* (1740). The name only became firmly popular in the 20th century.
Variant forms: **Pamala, Pamella** [pa-me-la].
Familiar form: **Pam.**

Pamella variant form of **Pamela.**

Pancras (m)
From Greek meaning 'ruler over all'. St Pancras was an early saint whose name survives in the name of a London railway station.

Pandora (f)
From Greek meaning 'every gift'. According to Greek myth, Pandora opened a chest which she had been forbidden to touch and thus released from it a torrent of sorrows and hardship into the world. In the *Diary of Adrian Mole* (1980) by Sue Townsend, Pandora is Adrian's girlfriend.

Pansy (f)
From the name of the flower, in use from the end of the 19th century, but never widely popular.

Paris (m)
From the name of the Trojan prince who caused the Trojan war by abducting the beautiful Helen from Greece. It is mainly used in the USA.
Variant form: **Parris.**

Parry (m)
From a Welsh surname, itself from **ap Harry** meaning 'son of Harry'
(See **Bevan**).

Pascal (m)
From French meaning 'connected with Easter'. Conferred by parents
on sons born at Easter.

Pascale female form of **Pascal**.

Pat familiar form of **Patricia**, **Patrick**.

Patience (f)
From the word 'patience' used as a name. The Puritans favoured the
use of virtues as names. Patience Strong was a 20th-century writer of
homely verse with a comforting message.

Patricia (f)
From Latin meaning 'noble'. Female form of **Patrick**. St Patricia was a
7th-century saint, but the name came into popular use in the 20th
century. It is enhanced in Ireland by association with St Patrick.
Familiar forms **Pat, Patsy, Pattie, Patti, Patty, Tricia, Trish, Trisha.**

Patrick (m)
From Irish Gaelic **Pádraig** which may be derived from Latin
Patricius, meaning 'noble man'. St Patrick was a 5th-century
missionary who became patron saint of Ireland. Its great popularity
in Ireland has only declined recently to give way to the Irish Gaelic
form of the name, **Pádraig**, has become increasingly popular since
1970.
Familiar forms: **Paddy, Pat, Patsy.**

Patsy familiar form of **Patricia** and **Patrick**.

Patti familiar form of **Patricia**.

Pattie familiar form of **Patricia**.

Patty familiar form of **Patricia**.

Paul (m)
Biblical, from Latin meaning 'small'. St Paul is the author of the part
of the New Testament known as the Epistles. The name has been
extremely popular in the 20th century and is borne by pop singer
Paul McCartney, actor Paul Newman, writer Paul Scott. The present
Pope is John Paul II.
Other forms: **Pól** (Irish Gaelic), **Pòl** (Scottish Gaelic).

Paula female form of Paul.

Pauleen variant form of **Pauline.**

Paulene variant form of **Pauline.**

Paulette French female diminutive of Paul.

Paulina (f)
From the female form of the Latin name **Paulinus**, itself from 'paulus'
meaning 'little.

Pauline (f)
The French form, now more commonly used in Britain than the
original English form, of **Paulina.**
Variant forms: **Paulene, Pauleen.**

Peadar Scottish and Irish Gaelic form of **Peter.**

Pearce variant form of **Piers.**

Pearl (f)
From the name of the gem. Rose Tremain, 20th-century novelist, used
the name for the beautiful girl in *Sacred Country.*
Variant form: **Pearle.**
Familiar forms **Pearly, Perly, Pearlie, Perlie.**

Pearle variant form of **Pearl.**

Peers variant form of **Piers.**

Peg familiar form of **Margaret.**

Peggie familiar form of **Margaret.**

Peggy familiar form of **Margaret**

Pelham (m)
From the surname, itself from a place name meaning 'Peola's place or settlement'. It was the first name of the humorous writer P G Wodehouse (1881-1975), author of many comic novels, including *What ho! Jeeves.*

Penelope (f)
From Greek meaning 'bobbin' and therefore connected with spinning. According to Greek legend, Penelope, wife of Odysseus, kept suitors away during her husband's absence with the excuse that she had to finish weaving a shroud for her father-in-law. At night she undid what she had woven by day .
Familiar forms: **Pennie, Penny.**

Pepita (f)
From the familiar form of the Spanish name **Josefina.** See **Josephine.**

Perce familiar form of **Percival, Percy.**

Percival (m)
Invented by the medieval poet, Chrétien de Troyes for a character who was supposed to be one of King Arthur's knights. Used in the 19th century, but uncommon since then.
Familiar form: **Perce.**

Percy (m)
From a surname, itself from a French place name. Percy Bysshe Shelley was one of the most distinguished bearers of the name which has not been popular since the 19th century.
Familiar form: **Perce.**

Perdita (f)
From Latin meaning 'lost', a name invented by Shakespeare for the baby princess disowned by her father Leontes in *A Winter's Tale.*

Peregrine (m)
From Latin meaning 'pilgrim'. Peregrine Pickle is the hero of Tobias
Smollet's novel of that name (1751). Peregrine Worsthorne is a well-
known 20th-century journalist.
Familiar form: **Perry**.

Perlie familiar form of **Pearl**.

Perly familiar form of **Pearl**.

Peronelle see **Petronella**.

Perry (m)
Familiar form of **Peregrine**, often used as a name in its own right.

Pet familiar form of **Peta, Petena, Peterina, Peternella, Petra, Petrina,
Petrona, Petronella, Petula**.

Peta (f)
Familiar female form of **Peter**.

Pete familiar form of **Peter**.

Petena (f)
Familiar female form of **Peter**.

Peter (m)
Biblical, from Greek meaning 'rock'. This was the word used to
translate the Aramaic name meaning 'rock' which Jesus gave to the
Apostle now known as Peter. *Peter Pan* (1904) by J M Barrie started
the 20th-century vogue for this name, borne by such film stars as
Peter O'Toole, Peter Ustinov, Peter Sellers.
Other forms: **Peadar** (Irish and Scottish Gaelic), **Pádraig** (Scottish
Gaelic [paa-drik]).
Familiar form: **Pete**.

Peterina female form of **Peter**.

Peternella female form of **Peter**, but possibly also derived from **Petronella**.

Petra female form of **Peter**.

Petrina female form of **Peter**.

Petrona (f)
Of uncertain origin, either a female form of **Peter** or derived from **Petronella**.
Familiar forms: **Pet, Rona, Rhona.**

Petronella (f)
From the Roman family name **Petronius**. St Petronella (sometimes spelt Petronilla) was said to be the daughter of St Peter.
Medieval form: **Peronelle**
Familiar form: **Pet.**

Petula (f)
From Latin meaning 'mischievous', but often considered to be a female form of **Peter**. The 20th-century actress Petula Clark, with her long career in the public eye, has made the name well known..
Familiar form: **Pet.**

Peyton (m)
From the surname, itself from place name meaning 'farm of Paega'.
The TV series named *Peyton Place* has made the name familiar.

Phebe variant form of **Phoebe**.

Phelan (m)
From Irish Gaelic meaning 'wolf'

Phemie familiar form of **Euphemia**.

Pheobe variant form of **Phoebe**.

Pheoby variant form of **Pheobe**.

Phil familiar form of **Philip, Phillippa, Philomena, Phyllis, Felicity.**

Philander (m)
From Greek meaning 'lover of men'. In Ariosto's *Orlando Furioso*,
Philander is trapped into killing Gabrina's husband and into
marrying her.

Philemon (m)
Biblical, from Greek meaning 'kiss'. In the New Testament, Philemon
is the person to whom St Paul wrote one of his epistles.

Philip (m)
Biblical, from Greek meaning 'lover of horses'. In the New Testament,
Philip is one of the twelve apostles. Prince Philip is the husband of
Queen Elizabeth II.
Variant form: **Phillip.**
Familiar forms: **Pip, Phil.**

Philipa variant form of **Phillippa.**

Philippa variant form of **Phillippa.**

Philis variant form of **Phyllis.**

Phillida variant form of **Phyllida.**

Phillie familiar form of **Phyllis, Phyllida, Philomena.**

Phillip variant form of **Philip.**

Phillippa (f)
Female form of **Philip.**
Variant forms: **Philipa, Phillipa, Philippa.**
Familiar forms: **Pip, Pippa, Phil, Phillie, Philly.**

Phillis variant form of **Phyllis.**

Philly familiar form of **Phyllis, Phyllida, Philomena.**

Philomena (f)
From Greek meaning 'beloved'. It was a popular name in the early Christian church, but little used afterwards until the 20th century.
Variant form: **Philomina.**
Familiar form: **Phil, Phillie, Philly.**

Phineas (m)
Biblical, of uncertain origin, possibly from Hebrew meaning 'oracle'. In the Old Testament it is the name of Aaron's grandson. Phineas Freak is a character in American cult comics of the 1990s.

Phoebe (f) [fee-bee]
From Greek meaning 'pure'. Phoebe was the Greek goddess of the moon.
Variant forms: **Phebe, Pheobe, Pheoby.**

Phyllida (f)
Originally a form of **Phyllis,** but used as a separate name from the 15th century onwards.
Variant form: **Phillida.**
Familiar forms: **Phil, Phillie, Philly.**

Phyllis (f)
From Greek meaning 'foliage'. According to Greek mythology, Phyllis was a country girl who was changed into a tree.
Variant forms **Philis, Phillis, Phyliss.**
Familiar forms: **Phil, Phillie, Philly.**

Piaras Irish Gaelic form of **Piers.**

Pierce variant form of **Piers.**

Piers (m)
A medieval form of **Peter.** The most famous example is in the 14th-century poem *Piers Plowman* by William Langland.
Variant forms: **Pearce, Pierce, Peers, Piaras** (Irish Gaelic).

Pip familiar form of **Philip.**

Pippa familiar form of **Phillippa.**

Piran (m)
From a Cornish place name, itself probably in origin a form of **Peter**.

Pol familiar form of **Polly**.

Pól Irish Gaelic form of **Paul**.

Pòl Scottish Gaelic form of **Paul**.

Poll familiar form of **Polly**.

Polly (f)
From **Molly**, in itself a pet form of **Mary** and long used as a name in its own right. It has been a favourite name in poetry and song, as in *Pretty little Polly Perkins* and *Polly put the kettle on*.
Variant form: **Pollie**.
Familiar forms: **Pol, Poll**.

Pollyanna (f)
A combination of **Polly** and **Anna**, invented by E H Porter in her children's novel *Pollyanna* about a girl renowned for her optimism.

Poppy (f)
From the name of the flower.

Portia (f)
From a Roman family name, itself from Latin meaning 'pig'. Portia is the beautiful heroine of Shakepeare's *The Merchant of Venice* .
Disguised as a male lawyer, she saves the life of Antonio by pleading for him in court.

Posie variant form of **Posy**.

Posy (f)
Possibly from a pleasing association with flower names, or a familiar form of **Josephine**. Posy Simmonds has been a successful cartoonist in the national press during the 1990s.
Variant form: **Posie**.

Preston (m)
From the surname, itself from the place name meaning 'priest's place'.

Price (m)
From the Welsh surname **ap Rhys** meaning 'son of **Rhys**'.

Primrose (f)
From the name of the flower, itself from Latin meaning 'first rose'.

Primula (f)
From Latin meaning 'first', also often connected with the flower of the primrose family.

Prince (m)
From the surname, itself from the royal title, indicating either that the family was of royal origin, or, more often that the original bearers had been in the service of a prince.

Princess (f)
From the royal title but very uncommon as a first name.

Priscilla (f)
From Latin meaning 'from ancient times'. Priscilla (Cilla) Black is a famous 20th-century singer and TV presenter. It is also the name of Elvis Presley's daughter.
Familiar forms: **Scilla, Cilla.**

Prosper (m)
From Latin meaning 'prosperous'. Many early saints bore this name.
Pru familiar form of Prudence, Prunella.

Prudence (f)
The word 'prudence' used as a name. Prudence Leith is a well known cookery writer.
Familiar forms: **Pru, Prue.**

Prunella (f)
From Latin meaning 'little plum'.
Familiar forms: **Pru, Prue.**

Pryderi (m) [prid-airy]
From Welsh meaning 'caring for'.

Queenie (f)
From Old English, meaning 'woman'and associated with the royal title.

Quentin (m)
Old French from a Latin name **Quintus**. St Quintus was a 3rd-century saint.
Variant form: **Quintin**. Quintin Hogg is the name of Viscount Hailsham, who, as a lawyer and politician, has been in public life for over fifty years.

Quincy (m)
From the French surname, itself from the Roman family name **Quintus** meaning fifth. Mainly used in North America. See also **Quentin**.

Quintin variant form of **Quentin**.

Rab familiar form of **Robert** in Scotland.

Rabbie familiar form of **Robert** in Scotland.

Rachael variant form of **Rachel**.

Rachel (f)
Biblical, from Hebrew meaning 'ewe'. In the Old Testament (Genesis 29-35), **Rachel** was the wife of Jacob. The name has been particularly popular in the 20th century. In the Scottish Highlands it has been used as an anglicized form of the Gaelic name **Raoghnald** [roe-nalt], itself from Norse **Ragnhildr**.
Other form: **Rachael, Rachelle, Raquel** (Spanish) [ra-kel].
Familiar forms: **Rae, Ray**.

Raghnall Gaelic form of **Ronald**.

Raibert Scottish Gaelic form of **Robert**.

Raina Russian form of **Regina**.

Raine variant form of **Raina**.

Ralph (m)
From Norman-French, based on a Germanic name meaning 'counsel' + 'wolf'. An earlier pronunciation was [rafe] which is still preferred by some people. The 20th-century actor Sir Ralph Richardson lent distinction to this already popular name.

Ramona (f)
Female form of **Ramón**, the Spanish form of **Raymond**. An early 20th-century song *Ramona* helped to popularize the name.

Ramsay (m)
From the Scottish surname, itself based on an English place name in Huntingdonshire, meaning 'garlic' + 'island'. In the 12th century, David I King of Scots owned lands in the east of England where he was brought up. On succeeeding to the Scottish throne, he took with him retainers with English surnames, such as Ramsay.

Ranald (m)
Anglicized form of the Scottish Gaelic name **Raghnall**.

Randal variant form of **Randall**.

Randall (m)
From the surname, itself a medieval form of **Randolph**.
Variant forms: **Randal, Randel, Randle.**

Randolph (m)
From Old English meaning 'shield' + 'wolf'. The name was known in the Middle Ages, but only taken up again in the 19th century. Randolph Churchill was the name of two politicians, father and son of the statesman Winston Churchill.

Raoghnald see **Rachel**.

Raphael (m)
Biblical, from Hebrew meaning 'God has healed'. In the Old
Testament, Raphael is the name of one of the archangels. Little used
in the 20th century.

Raquel Spanish form of **Rachel**.

Ray (m and f)
Familiar form of **Raymond** and **Rachel**, used as a name in its own
right.

Raymond (m)
Norman-French of Germanic origin meaning 'counsel' + 'protection'.
A favourite name at the start of the 20th century.
Familiar form: **Ray**.

Rayner (m)
Norman-French of Germanic origin meaning 'decision' + 'army'.

Rebecca (f)
Biblical, possibly from Hebrew or Aramaic meaning 'binding'. In the
Old Testament, Rebecca is the mother of Jacob and Esau (Genesis 24–
28). The name's consistent popularity was increased with the book
and film of Daphne du Maurier's novel *Rebecca* (1940).
Variant form: **Rebekah.**
Familiar form: **Becky.**

Reenie familiar form of **Renée.**

Reece variant form of **Rhys.**

Rees variant form of **Rhys.**

Reg familiar form of **Reginald.**

Regan (f)
Of uncertain origin, possibly invented by Shakespeare, it is the name
of one of the three daughters in *King Lear* (1605). Some modern users
associate it with the Irish surname **Regan** or **Reagan.**

Reggie familiar form of **Reginald**.

Regina (f) [rej-ee-na, rej-eye-na]
From Latin meaning 'queen'.
Other forms: **Raina** (Russian), **Raine**.
Familiar form: **Gina**.

Reginald (m)
From Germanic meaning 'decision' + 'ruler'. In the Middle Ages, the usual form was **Reynold**, which reflects the normal pronunciation at the time. The name has declined in popularity.
Familiar forms: **Reg, Reggie**.

Rena variant form of **Rina** or of **Renée**.

Renée (f)
French from Latin meaning 'reborn'.
Variant forms: **Reenie** (indicating the usual English pronunciation), **Rena**.

Reuben (m)
Biblical, from Hebrew meaning 'behold a son'. In the Old Testament (Genesis 29:31), Reuben was the son of Jacob who gave his name to one of the tribes of Israel.
Variant forms: **Ruben**.

Rex (m)
From Latin meaning 'king'.

Reynold see **Reginald**.

Rhian (f) [ree-an]
From Welsh meaning 'maiden'.
Variant form: **Rhianu** [ree-an].

Rhiannon (f) [ree-an-on]
From Welsh meaning 'goddess'.
Other form: **Rona**.

Rhianu variant form of **Rhian**.

Rhoda (f)
From Greek meaning 'rose'.

Rhona (f)
Possibly from the name of the island of Rona in the Hebrides. If so, the 'h' may have been inserted to bring the spelling into line with Rhoda. Also spelt **Rona.**

Rhys (m) [rhymes with 'peace']
From Welsh meaning 'ardour'. A favourite name in Wales.
Variant form: **Rees, Reece.**

Rica familiar form of **Frederica, Erica.**

Richard (m)
From Germanic meaning 'strong ruler'. Introduced into England by William the Conqueror in the 11th century and one of the most well-used names for centuries. Famous Richards include three kings of England and a number of 20th-century actors, such as Richard Burton and Richard Chamberlain.
Familiar forms: **Dick, Dickie, Dicky, Rick, Rickie, Ricky.**

Richmal (f)
From a combination of **Richard** and **Michael** . Uncommon except for the well-known example of Richmal Crompton, the 20th-century children's writer who created the *William* stories.

Rick familiar form of **Richard.**

Rickie familiar form of **Richard.**

Ricky familiar form of **Richard.**

Ridley (m)
From the surname, itself based on a place name meaning 'reeds' + 'clearing'.

Rika familiar form of **Frederica, Erica.**

Rina (f)
Familiar form of **Katarina** or other name with this ending.
Variant form: **Rena**.

Rita (f)
Originally from a familiar form of **Margherita** (see **Margaret**), but its
links are forgotten and it is used in its own right as a popular name.
St Rita (1380-1457) is the patron saint of unhappy marriages and
desperate cases, having suffered a violent husband and quarrelling
sons before she became a nun.

Rob familiar form of **Robert**.

Robbie familiar form of **Robert**.

Robby familiar form of **Robert**.

Robert (m)
From Old English meaning 'fame' + 'bright'. Enthusiasm for this
name dates from the Norman Conquest until today. The list of
famous bearers is striking, from Robert the Bruce of Scotland, king
and hero, to the poet Robert Burns, American politician Robert
Kennedy, and actor Robert Redford. See also **Robin**.
Familiar forms: **Rab, Rabbie** (Scottish), **Rob, Robbie, Bob, Bobby,
Bobbie, Bert, Bertie**.
Other forms: **Rupert** (German), **Raibeart** (Scottish Gaelic) [raa-bert],
Roibeard (Irish Gaelic) [ri-**board**].

Roberta (f)
Female form of **Robert**.
Familiar form: **Bobbie, Bobby**.

Robin (m and f)
Originally a familiar form of **Robert**, but long separated from it and
used as a name in its own right, particularly in Scotland. As a female
name, it appeared in the 20th century associated with the bird
name.The most famous bearer of the male name was Robin Hood.
Variant forms: **Robyn, Robynne**.

Rocco see **Rocky**.

Rocky (m)
From an American nickname for a hard fearless person. It came to
prominence with the boxer Rocky Marciano (1923-1969). He
anglicized his Italian name **Rocco** to suggest his toughness.

Rod familiar forms of **Roderick, Rodney.**

Roddy familiar forms of **Roderick, Rodney.** Roddy Doyle is a well
known Irish writer.

Roderick (m)
Of Germanic origin meaning 'fame' + 'rule'.The name was favoured
by writers in the past, as in Tobias Smollett's *Roderick Random* (1748),
Sir Walter Scott's *The Vision of Don Roderick* (1811). Not common,
except in the Scottish Highlands, where it is used as an anglicized
version of the unrelated Gaelic name **Ruaraidh** (see **Rory**).
Familiar forms: **Rod, Roddy.**

Rodger variant form of **Roger.**

Rodney (m)
From the surname, itself based on the place name, meaning 'reed' +
'island'. Began to be used as a first name in the mid 19th century, but
declined after the 1950s. Sir Arthur Conan Doyle's *Rodney Stone*
appeared at the height of the name's popularity in 1896.
Familiar forms: **Rod, Roddy.**

Roger (m)
Norman-French of Germanic origin meaning 'fame' + 'spear'. A
popular name from the Middle Ages onwards, but much less so in
the 20th century, although Roger Moore, hero of the James Bond
films, has given the name a modern flavour. Also Roger Daltry is a
famous rock musician of the 1990s.
Variant form: **Rodger.**

Rohan (m)
From the Irish surname , probably from Irish Gaelic, meaning 'red'.
Other form: **Rowan.**

Roibeard Irish Gaelic form of **Robert**.

Róisín (f) [ro-sheen]
From Irish Gaelic meaning 'little rose'.
Variant form: **Rosheen** (anglicized).

Roland (m)
Norman-French of Germanic origin, probably meaning 'famous land'. A famous name from the Middle Ages onwards because of the exploits of a legendary hero at Charlemagne's court, written about by many writers, including the medieval French *Chanson de Roland* and the Italian Renaissance *Orlando Furioso* of Ariosto. Much less used in the 20th century.
Familiar form: **Roly**.

Rolf Scandinavian and German form of **Rudolph**.

Roly familiar form of **Roland**.

Ron familiar form of **Ronald**.

Rona variant form of **Rhona**.

Ronald (m)
From an Old Norse form of the name **Reynold**, meaning 'counsel' + 'power'. It has long been popular throughout the English-speaking world. Ronald Reagan, actor turned politician, was president of the USA from 1980 to 1988.
Other form: **Raghnall** (Scottish Gaelic).
Familiar forms: **Ron, Ronnie**.

Rónán (m) [roa-nan]
From Irish Gaelic meaning 'little seal'.
Other form: **Ronan** (anglicized).

Rory (m)
Anglicized form of Scottish Gaelic **Ruaridh** and Irish Gaelic **Ruairí** meaning 'red'. Common in Scotland where this Gaelic name is sometimes anglicized as **Roderick**.

Ros familiar form of **Rosalind** or **Rosamund.**

Rosa a variant form of **Rose.**

Rosaleen variant form of **Rosalind,** or used as an anglicized variant of Irish Gaelic **Róisín.**

Rosalie (f)
From a French name based on Latin meaning 'rose'. St Rosalie is the patron saint of Palermo in Sicily.

Rosalind (f)
Norman-French of Germanic origin probably meaning 'horse' + 'tender'. In the Middle Ages, it was associated with Latin words meaning 'rose' + 'lovely'; and today also the preference is to connect its meaning to 'rose'. Rosalind is the heroine of Shakespeare's *As you like It.*
Variant forms: **Rosaleen, Rosaline, Rosalyn.**
Familiar forms: **Ros, Roz.**

Rosaline variant form of **Rosalind.**

Rosalyn variant form of **Rosalind.**

Rosamond variant form of **Rosamund.**

Rosamund (f)
Norman-French of Germanic origin meaning 'horse' + 'protection', but, as with many 'rose' names, people have preferred to search for a connection with the flower. Thus, it is sometimes considered to be from Latin meaning 'rose of the world'.
Variant form: **Rosamond.**
Familiar forms: **Ros, Roz.**

Rosanne (f)
From a combination of **Rose** and **Anne**. Rosanne Barr is an American 20th-century actor.
Variant forms: **Roseanne, Rozanne.**

Rose (f)
From the name of the flower. Common long before flower names came into popular use in the 19th century. Probably from Germanic names, based on words meaning 'horse', an important feature of the life of Germanic tribes. However, the English flower name is a more attractive association for most people.
Variant form: **Rosa**.

Roseanne variant form of **Rosanne**.

Rosemary (f)
From Latin meaning 'sea dew'. However, some people choose to derive it from the combined names **Rose** and **Mary**. Others like the association with the fragrant, blue-flowered rosemary plant.

Rosheen anglicized form of **Róisín**.

Ross (m)
From the surname, itself of various different origins, including a Celtic place name element, meaning 'headland, promontory'.

Rowan (m and f)
As a female name, from the tree name. As a male name, variant form of **Rohan**.

Rowena (f)
Latinized form of a Saxon name, itself probably from Germanic meaning 'fame' + 'joy'.

Roxane (f)
Probably of Persian origin, meaning 'dawn'.

Roxanne variant form of **Roxane**.

Roy (m)
From Scottish Gaelic *ruadh* meaning 'red'. Not popular since the 1950s. Politicians Roy Hattersley and Roy Jenkins are well known 20th-century bearers of the name. It is also used as a short form of names such as **Leroy**, **Delroy** from Old French *roy* meaning 'king'.

Roz familiar form of **Rosalind** or **Rosamund.**

Rozanne variant form of **Rosanne.**

Ruaraidh see **Rory.**

Ruarí see **Rory.**

Ruben variant form of **Reuben.**

Ruby (f)
From the name of the red jewel. Ruby Wax is a television star famous in 20th century Britain and the USA.

Rudolf variant form of **Rudolph.**

Rudolph (m)
From Germanic meaning 'fame' + 'wolf'. Romantic film star Rudolph Valentino in the 1920s and later Rudolph Nureyev, the ballet dancer, brought prestige to the name, but it was also diminished by the popular song *Rudolf the red-nosed reindeer.*
Other forms: **Rolf** (Scandinavian and German), **Rudolf.**
Familiar forms: **Rudy, Rudi.**

Rupert (m)
A German form of **Robert**. It was was brought to England by Prince Rupert of the Rhine, a nephew of Charles I, who helped to lead the Royalist army in the Civil War. Rupert Brooke was one of the best-known poets of the First World War.

Russ familiar form of **Russell.**

Russel variant form of **Russell.**

Russell (m)
From the surname, of Norman-French origin, itself probably from a nickname meaning 'redhead'.
Variant form: **Russel.**
Familiar form: **Russ.**

Ruth (f)
Biblical, from Hebrew meaning 'friend'. In the Old Testament, the
Book of Ruth tells of Ruth's loyalty to Naomi, her mother-in-law.
Consistently popular, this name is also a favourite of writers,
including William Wordsworth, Mrs Gaskell and Felicia Hemans,
who chose it for their heroines.

Ryan (m)
From a common Irish surname of uncertain origin, perhaps meaning
'little king', or from the name of an ancient sea or river god, as in the
name of the River Rhine. The 20th-century film star Ryan O'Neill and
the Manchester United footballer, Ryan Giggs brought the first name
into the top ten in popularity in 1995.

Sabina (f)
From the name of a tribe, the Sabines, whose women were abducted
by the Romans in central Italy. St Sabina was an early Christian.

Sabrina (f)
From the Roman name of the English River Severn. According to
Celtic legend, the river is called after Sabrina, daughter of a Welsh
King and his mistress. When the Queen discovered the child, she
drowned her in the river.

Sadie (f)
Familiar form of **Sarah**, long used as a name in its own right.

Saffrey (f)
Possibly from **Saffron**. It may also be associated with **Affery**. See
Aphra.

Saffron (f)
From the name of a special, highly-prized, white crocus, used to
colour food yellow.

Sal familiar form of **Sally, Sarah.**

Sally (f)
Originally a familiar form of **Sarah**, but long used as a name in its
own right and often combined with other names, as in **Sally-Anne.**

Familiar form: **Sal.**

Sam familiar form of **Samuel, Samson** or **Samantha.**

Samantha (f)
Originally a female form of Samuel, used in the Southern states of the America in the 18th century. Various Samanthas in film and television have made the name fashionable in Britain and the USA in the 20th century. The heroine of the 1960s TV serial *Bewitched* was a beautiful witch called Samantha.
Familiar forms: **Sam, Sammie, Sammy.**

Sammie, Sammy familiar forms of **Samuel, Samantha, Samson.**
Sammy Davis Junior is a famous musician.

Sampson variant form of **Samson.**

Samson (m)
Biblical, from Hebrew probably meaning 'sun'. In the Old Testament Samson was betrayed to the Philistines by his mistress Delilah. He was captured, but brought down the pillars of the temple on himself and his enemies(Judges 13-16).
Variant form: **Sampson.**
Familiar forms: **Sam, Sammie, Sammy.**

Samuel (m)
Biblical, from Hebrew meaning possibly 'requested of God'. In the Old Testament, Samuel, a judge and a prophet, has two books named after him. Famous writers bearing the name were Samuel Johnson, Samuel Taylor Coleridge and Samuel Pepys.
Familiar forms: **Sam, Sammie, Sammy.**

Sandie familiar form of **Alexandra** or **Alexander.**

Sandra (f)
Familiar form of **Alexandra** used as a name in its own right.

Sandy familiar form of **Alexandra** or **Alexander.**

Sapphire (f)
From the name of the blue gemstone, itself derived ultimately from
Greek meaning 'lapis lazuli'.

Sara variant form of **Sarah**.

Sarah (f)
Biblical, from Hebrew meaning 'princess'. In the Old Testament,
Sarah was the wife of Abraham (Genesis 20-23). Widely used over the
last four centuries.
Variant form: **Sara**.
Familiar forms: **Sally, Sadie, Sal**.

Saul (m)
Biblical, from Hebrew meaning 'prayed for'. Saul was the first king of
the Israelites and father-in-law of David. In the New Testament, it
was the name of the apostle Paul before his conversion. A famous
modern bearer is the 20th-century American writer Saul Bellow.

Scarlet variant form of **Scarlett**.

Scarlett (f)
From the surname, itself from the Old French name for a dyer or
seller of rich fabrics. It is the name of the heroine of *Gone with the
Wind* by Margaret Mitchell (1936).
Variant form: **Scarlet**.

Scilla familiar form of **Priscilla**.

Scott (m)
From the surname, meaning a Scotsman. Scott Joplin was a famous
American ragtime musician (1868-1917) and Scott Fitzgerald a
famous American writer (1896-1940). The name became popular in
Britain in the 1950s.

Séamas [shay-mus] Irish Gaelic form of **James**. Frequently spelt
Seamus.

Seán [shawn] Irish Gaelic form of **John**. The Scottish actor Sean Connery changed his name from Thomas to Sean. Frequently spelt without the accent. See also **Shane, Shaun**.

Sebastian (m)
From the name of a city in Asia Minor. St Sebastian was a 3rd-century soldier in the Roman army who was martyred for his faith. Traditionally he was portrayed in painting as a beautiful youth pierced by arrows.

Selena variant form of **Selina**.

Selina (f)
From Greek after Selene, the Moon goddess.
Variant form: **Selena**.

Selma (f)
Originally a familiar form of **Anselma**, itself a female form of **Anselm**, used as a name in its own right.

Selwyn (m)
From Latin meaning 'of the woods'. It can also be interpreted as deriving from Welsh meaning 'ardour' + 'fair'.

Senga (f)
From **Agnes**, spelt back to front. Occasionally used in Scotland.

Seònag Scottish Gaelic form of **Joan**.

Seònaid Scottish Gaelic form of **Janet**.

Seonaidh see **John**.

Seoirse Irish Gaelic form of **George**.

Seòras Scottish Gaelic form of **George**.

Septimus (m)
From the Latin word for 'seven'. Rare in the 20th century.

Serena (f)
From Latin meaning 'calm'. It was the name of an early saint.

Seth (m)
Biblical, from Hebrew meaning 'to fix or appoint'. In the Old
Testament, Seth was the third son of Adam and Eve (Genesis 4:25).
Seth is a humorous, but likeable character in Stella Gibbons' *Cold
Comfort Farm* (1933).

Seumas Scottish Gaelic form of James.

Shane (m and f)
An Anglicized form of **Seán** which reflects the Northern Irish
pronunciation of that Irish Gaelic name.

Shannon (f)
From the name of the Irish river. It is little used in Ireland, but
popular in the USA and increasingly in Britain.

Sharan variant form of **Sharon**.

Sharman (m and f)
From the surname and also from a variant form of **Charmian**.

Sharon (f)
Biblical, from Hebrew meaning 'a plain'. In the Old Testament, it is
mentioned as the plain between Jaffa and Mount Carmel, not as a
personal name. In the *Song of Songs*, a certain beautiful woman is
called the Rose of Sharon. Popular in the mid 1960s.
Variant form: **Sharan**.

Shaun Anglicized form of Irish Gaelic **Seán** and the most used
spelling in England.
Variant form: **Shawn**.

Sheba familiar form of **Bathsheba**.

Sheelagh variant form of **Sheila**.

Sheena see Jean.

Sheila (f)
From the Irish Gaelic name Síle, itself a form of **Celia** or **Cecelia**. In Australia, **Sheila** is slang for 'girl', but it may have a different origin. Variant forms: **Sheelagh, Shiela.**

Shelley (m and f)
From the surname, itself from various place names, meaning 'meadow above a cliff or slope'. The name was used for boys in the 19th century, but in the 20th has gradually become a girl's name, perhaps because of its similarity to Shirley and from the example of the actress Shelley Winters.

Sheree other form of **Chérie.**

Sheridan (m)
From the Irish surname, made famous by the playwright Richard Brinsley Sheridan (1751-1816).

Sherman (m)
From the surname, itself from Old English meaning 'shears' + 'man' meaning 'man who trims the nap from woven cloth'.

Sherry variant form of **Chérie.**

Sheryl variant form of **Cheryl.**

Shiela variant form of **Sheila.**

Shirl familiar form of **Shirley.**

Shirley (f)
From the surname, itself a place name from Old English meaning 'bright meadow'. Shirley is the heroine of Charlotte Bronte's novel *Shirley* (1849) based on her own life. The child film star Shirley Temple boosted the popularity of the name in the 1930s. Familiar form: **Shirl.**

Shona (f)
Anglicized form of Scottish Gaelic **Seònaid.** See **Janet.**

Variant form: **Shonagh.**

Shug, Shuggie Scottish familiar forms of **Hugh.**

Shula (f)
From Hebrew, meaning 'peace' and probably derived from the current Hebrew name **Shulamit** which is not used as an English name. The Radio 4 serial *The Archers* has a character called Shula.

Sian [shahn] Welsh form of **Jane.**

Sid familiar form of **Sidney**

Sidney (m)
From the surname, itself probably from two different sources, depending on the origin of the family. In some cases, Sidney is from a place name, itself from Old English, meaning 'wide water meadow', in others, from the French place name, St Denis. It has occasionally been used as a female name, possibly confused with the French **Sidonie.**
Variant form: **Sydney.**
Familiar form: **Sid.**

Sidonie variant form of **Sidony.**

Sidony (f) [sid-on-ee]
From Latin meaning 'a person from Sidon'(the Phoenician city).
Variant form: **Sidonie** (French).

Silas (m)
From a Greek form of a Latin name **Silvanus** meaning 'one who lives in the woods'. It is mentioned in the New Testament (Acts 15:22). Little used in the 20th century, but well known as the title of George Eliot's *Silas Marner* about a miser who is redeemed through the love of a child.

Sile see Celia, Sheila.

Silvester (m)
From Latin meaning, 'of the woods'. As St Silvester was an early

martyr, popes were called after him and early Christians often took
the name. It is rare in the 20th century and the actor Sylvester
Stallone is an unusual bearer of the name.
Variant form: **Sylvester.**
Familiar form: **Sly.** Sly Stone and Sly Dunbar are famous pop
musicians.

Silvia (f)
From Latin meaning 'wood'. Writers have long been fond of this
name for their characters. Shakespeare uses it in *Two Gentlemen of
Verona* (1594).
Variant form: **Sylvia.**

Simeon (m)
Biblical, from Hebrew meaning 'listening'. It is considered to be
closer to the Hebrew form of the name rendered as **Simon** in English.
In the New Testament (Luke 2:25) Simeon was the priest who blessed
the infant Jesus in the temple.

Simon (m)
The preferred English form of the Hebrew name **Simeon**. It appears
frequently in the New Testament, including two apostles.
Other form: **Simeon** (Hebrew).

Simone (f)
French female form of **Simon.**

Sinclair (m)
From the Scottish surname, itself from a French place name. The
writer Sinclair Lewis (1885-1951) was a well- known bearer of the
name.

Sindy variant form of **Cindy.**

Síne Scottish Gaelic form of **Jean.**

Sinéad Irish Gaelic form of **Janet**

Siobhán Irish Gaelic form of **Jane.**

Sior Welsh form of **George**.

Siorys Welsh form of **George**.

Siùsaidh Scottish Gaelic form of **Susan**.

Sly familiar form of **Silvester**.

Sofia Italian and Scandinavian form of **Sophia**.

Sol familiar form of **Solomon**.

Solly familiar form of **Solomon**.

Solomon (m)
Biblical, from Hebrew meaning 'peace'. In the Old Testament (Samuel, Kings and Chronicles) Solomon is the wise king, son of David and Bathsheba. Mainly used by Jews.
Familiar forms: **Sol**, **Solly**.

Sonia (f)
From a familiar form of the Russian version of **Sophia**.
Variant form: **Sonya**.

Sophia (f)
From Greek meaning 'wisdom'. In this century, Sophia Loren, film actress, has given the name prestige.
Other forms: **Sophie** (French), **Sofia** (Scandinavian and Italian).

Sorcha (f) [sore-kha]
From Irish Gaelic meaning 'bright, radiant'.

Sorel variant form of **Sorrel**.

Sorell variant form of **Sorrel**.

Sorrel (f)
From the name of the edible plant with sour-tasting leaves, itself from Old French meaning 'sour.'
Variant forms: **Sorel**, **Sorell**, **Sorrell**.

Sorrell variant form of **Sorrel**.

Spencer (m)
From the surname, which derives from the occupation of a spencer, a kind of butler or steward. It is the name of the Earls of Spencer, the family of Princess Diana and the second name of Winston Churchill. Spencer Tracy (1900-1967) was a film star.

Spike (m)
From the nickname meaning 'a tuft of hair'. It is sometimes used as a first name after the comedian Spike Milligan or the musician Spike Jones.

Stacie variant form of **Stacey**.

Stacey (m and f)
As a male name, probably from a short form of **Eustace**; and as a female name, a short form of **Anastasia**. Now it is used as a name in its own right, more for girls than boys, with little remembered association with the original names.
Variant forms: **Stacy, Stacie**.

Stan familiar form of **Stanley**.

Stanley (m)
From the surname, itself based on a place name, from Old English meaning 'stony meadow'. It came into very popular use as a first name in the 1890s and remained so for about 50 years. Stanley Matthews was a famous soccer player and Stan Laurel a famous comic actor.
Familiar form: **Stan**.

Stef familiar form of **Stephanie**.

Stefanie variant form of **Stephanie**.

Steffie familiar form of **Stephanie**.

Stella (f)
From Latin meaning 'star', it was first used in the 16th century by the poet Sir Philip Sidney.

Stephanie (f)
Female form of **Stephen**, taken from the French form of the name.
Variant form: **Stefanie**.
Familiar forms: **Stef, Steffie**.

Stephen (m)
From Greek meaning 'crown'. St Stephen was a 1st-century martyr in Jerusalem, stoned to death for his faith. His name was adopted by many early Christians. His feast day is 26th December. In the Middle Ages Stephen became a popular name and has remained so.
Familiar form: **Steve, Stevie**.
Variant form: **Steven**, reflecting its pronunciation, **Stiofán** (Irish).

Steve, Stevie familiar forms of **Stephen**.

Stew familiar form of **Stuart**.

Stewart variant form of **Stuart**.

Stu familiar form of **Stuart**.

Stuart (m)
From the Scottish surname, itself from Old English meaning 'keeper of a household or estate'. It was the name of a line of Scottish kings and later of kings of the United Kingdom. This spelling is the French version used by Mary Stuart, Queen of Scots. Originally a Scottish first name, it is now widely used.
Variant form: **Stewart**.
Familiar forms: **Stu, Stew**.

Sue familiar form of **Susan**.

Susan (f)
Biblical, from Hebrew meaning 'lily'. A form of **Susannah** which has far exceeded the original in popularity. In the Old Testament in

Apocrypha, the beautiful Susannah was falsely accused of infidelity, but her accusers were caught out and punished.
Other forms: **Susannah** (Old Testament version), **Siùsaidh** (Scottish Gaelic [shoo-see]), **Suzanne** (French).
Familar forms: **Sue, Susie, Suzie, Suzy, Zana.**

Suzanne variant form of **Susan.**

Suzie, Suzy familiar forms of **Susan.**

Sybil (f)
From the Greek name for divinely inspired prophetesses. Benjamin Disraeli chose the name for the heroine of his novel *Sybil* (1845).
Sydney variant form of **Sidney.**

Sylvester variant form of **Silvester.**

Sylvia variant form of **Silvia.**

Tabatha variant form of **Tabitha.**

Tabitha (f)
Biblical from Aramaic, meaning 'gazelle'. In the New Testament (Acts 9). **Tabitha** is the woman raised from the dead by Peter. Little used this century.
Variant form: **Tabatha.**

Tadg variant form of **Tadhg.**

Tadhg (m) [tie-g]
From Irish Gaelic meaning 'poet',it was the name of several Irish kings and saints, as well as of a 16th-century poet.
Other forms: **Tadg, Teague** (anglicized).

Talfryn (m) [tal-frin]
From Welsh meaning 'high hill'.

Taliesin (m) [tal-ee-ess-in]
From Welsh meaning 'brow' + 'shining'. It was the name of a 6th-century Welsh poet.

Tallulah (f)
From the place name Tallulah Falls, itself from North American
Indian meaning 'spring water'. Tallulah Bankhead (1903-1968) was
an American actress.The name is also sometimes considered to be a
variant form of **Talulla.**

Talulla (f)
From Irish Gaelic meaning 'abundance' + 'lady or princess'. It was
the name of two early Irish saints.

Tam Scottish familiar form of **Thomas.**

Tamar variant form of **Tamara.**

Tamara (f)
From a Russian name, itself from a Biblical name, **Tamar** (Samuel
14:27) from Hebrew, meaning 'date palm'. Tamara was a 12th-
century Queen of Georgia and much written about in Russian
literature.
Other form: **Tamar** (Hebrew).
Familiar form: **Tammie, Tammy.**

Tammy, Tammie familiar forms of **Tamara** or, in Scotland, of
Thomas.

Tamsin (f)
Originally a familiar form of **Thomasina** in the Middle Ages,
persisting into modern times only in Cornwall, until it came into
fashion again in the 1950s. See **Thomas** and **Thomasina.**

Tania variant form of **Tanya.**

Tansy (f)
From the name of a yellow flower with a strong perfume, derived
from Greek meaning 'immortality'. Many writers, including T
Edwardes, author of *Tansy* (1921), have used the name.

Tanya (f)
Familiar form of **Tatiana,** used as an independent name .

Variant form: **Tania**.

Tara (f)
From Irish Gaelic **Teamhair**, possibly meaning 'hill'. The name has romantic connotations, as Tara was the legendary dwelling of the Irish kings.

Tarquin (m)
From Etruscan of uncertain meaning. It was borne by two early kings of Rome. Many Roman surnames derive from Etruscan.

Tasha familiar form of **Natasha**.

Tatiana (f)
From the Russian name, of uncertain origin.
Familiar forms: **Tanya, Tania**.

Tayler variant form of **Taylor**.

Taylor (m and f)
From the occupational surname, formerly only a male first name, now also female.
Variant form: **Tayler**.

Teague anglicized form of Irish Gaelic **Tadhg**.

Ted, Teddy, familiar forms of **Edward** and **Theodore**.

Tel familiar form of **Terence**.

Terence (m)
Derived from two different sources, (1) The English derivation is from a Roman family name, **Terentius**, (2) In Ireland it is considered to be the anglicized version of an Irish Gaelic name, meaning 'one who initiates an idea'.
Familiar form: **Terry, Tel**.

Teresa (f)
From Greek, either from the name of the island of Thera, or from a word meaning 'harvest'. **Teresa** is the most common spelling in most

of the British Isles, but in Ireland and the USA, **Theresa** is the preferred form. St Teresa of Avila (1515-1582) was a mystic, a reformer and influential writer.
Other forms: **Theresa** (Irish), **Thérèse** (French).
Familiar forms: **Terry, Terri, Teri, Tess, Tessa, Tessie, Tessy,Tracy.**

Terry (m and f)
Used as a name, in its own right, it is also a familiar form of the male name **Terence** and the female name **Teresa**. As an independent name it is probably from the surname, originally Norman-French, perhaps meaning 'tribal power'.

Tertius (m)
From Latin, meaning 'third'. It is the name of the doctor in George Eliot's *Middlemarch* (1871).

Tess familiar form of **Teresa**.

Tessa familiar form of **Teresa**.

Tessie familiar form of **Teresa**.

Tessy familiar form of **Teresa**.

Tex (m)
Originally a nickname for someone from Texas, but occasionally used as a a name in its own right after the example of Tex Ritter an early 20th-century American film star.

Thalia (f)[thay-lee-a]
From Greek meaning 'to flourish'.

Thea familiar form of **Dorothea**.

Thelma (f)
A name invented by Marie Corelli for the heroine of *Thelma* (1887), perhaps from a Greek word meaning 'wish' or 'will'. Name of a character in the film *Thelma and Louise*.

Theo (m)
Familiar form of **Theodore** or **Theobald**, now used as a name in its own right.

Theobald (m)
From Norman-French of Germanic origin meaning 'race' + 'brave'. Familiar form: **Theo.**

Theodora (f)
Female form of **Theodore**. It derives from the same Greek elements as **Dorothea**, which also means 'God's gift' and repeats them in reverse order.

Theodore (m)
From Greek, meaning 'God's gift'. Little used in the 20th century. The term 'teddy bear' derives from the familiar form of the name of the American president,Theodore Roosevelt (1858-1919). Familiar forms: **Theo, Ted, Teddy.**

Theodoric (m)
From Germanic meaning 'ruler of the people' but little used except in its familiar forms.
Familar forms: **Derek, Derrick,** now infinitely more popular than the original.

Theresa variant form of **Teresa.**

Thérèse French form of **Teresa,** used by some Catholics in honour of St Thérèse of Lisieux.

Thomas (m)
Biblical, from Aramaic, meaning 'twin'. In the New Testament, the apostle Thomas is referred to as having a twin. In the Middle Ages, it became popular and has been common ever since with many famous bearers, such as saints Thomas à Beckett (1118-1170) and St Thomas More (1478-1535)
Other forms: **Tomas** (Scottish Gaelic), **Tomás** (Irish Gaelic).
Familiar forms:Tom, Tommy, Tam, Tammy, Tammie (last three Scottish).

Thomasina (f)
Female form of **Thomas,** well-used in past centuries, but out of
fashion in the 20th century.
Other form: **Tamsin,** now much more popular than the original form.

Thora (f)
Probably from a Scandinavian name meaning 'battle of Thor', well-
known because of the 20th-century actress Thora Hird.

Tiarnan (m)
From Irish Gaelic meaning 'lord'.
Other form: **Tiernan.**

Tibbie familiar form of **Isabel.**

Tiffany (f)
From the surname, itself from Greek meaning 'epiphany' or
'showing' as in the name of the Christian feast of the Epiphany on
January 6th which commemorates the appearance of the child Jesus
in the Temple. Once common as a first name, it lost popularity until
the 1960s.

Tilda familiar form of **Mathilda.**

Tillie familiar form of **Mathilda.**

Tilly familiar form of **Mathilda.**

Tim familiar form of **Timothy.**

Timmie familiar form of **Timothy.**

Timmy familiar form of **Timothy.**

Timothy (m)
Biblical, from Greek meaning 'honouring God'. In the New
Testament, **Timothy** has two books, Epistles 1 and 2, addressed to
him by St Paul.
Familiar form: **Tim, Timmy, Timmie.**

Tina (f)
Familiar form of many names ending in -*ina*, such as **Christina**; also used as a name in its own right. Tina Turner is a famous pop singer.

Tirion (f)
From Welsh meaning 'kind and gentle'.

Tisha familiar form of **Letitia**.

Titus (m)
From a Roman first name of uncertain origin.

Tobias (m)
Biblical, from Hebrew meaning 'God is good'. In the Book of Tobit (Apocrypha), Tobias, son of Tobit, travelled far from home, was helped by an angel and returned a wealthy man.
Familiar form: **Toby.**

Tom (m)
Familiar form of **Thomas**, also used as a name in its own right.

Tomas Scottish Gaelic form of **Thomas**.

Tomás Irish Gaelic form of **Thomas**.

Tommy familiar form of **Thomas**, also used as a name in its own right.

Toni familiar form of **Antonia**.

Tony (m)
Familiar form of **Antony**, also used as a name in its own right.

Topaz (f)
From the name of the white gemstone.

Torcal Scottish Gaelic form of **Torquil**.

Torcul Scottish Gaelic form of **Torquil**.

Torquil (m)[tor-kwil or torkle]
From Old Norse, meaning 'the god Thor' and possibly 'cauldron'.
Mainly used in Scotland, especially by the Macleods of Lewis. It was
the name of the founder of that branch of the clan.
Other forms: **Torcal, Torcul** (both Scottish Gaelic).

Tory familiar form of **Victoria**.

Tracey variant form of **Tracy**.

Tracie variant form of **Tracy**.

Tracy (m and f)
From the Norman-French surname, itself from several similar place
names in France. Originally a male name, it is almost always a female
name in the 20th century. It is sometimes regarded as a familiar form
of **Teresa**. It was much favoured after two versions of the film *The
Philadelphia Story*, about the heiress, Tracy Lord, were shown in the
1940s and 50s.
Variant forms: **Tracey, Tracie**.

Trefor Welsh form of **Trevor**.

Trev familiar form of **Trevor**.

Trevor (m)
From the surname, itself from a Welsh place name in Caernarvon,
Denbigh and Anglesea, meaning 'big settlement or village'. Its use as
a first name started in the mid 1860s and remained popular, helped
by the fame of actor Trevor Howard.
Other form: **Trefor** (Welsh).
Familiar form: **Trev**.

Tricia familiar form of **Patricia**.

Trish familiar form of **Patricia**.

Trisha familiar form of **Patricia**.

Tristan Welsh, German and French form of **Tristram**.

Tristram (m)
From Celtic meaning 'din, tumult'. It is the English version of the
hero's name in the medieval tragic tale of *Tristan and Isolde*. They fell
in love, although Isolde was betrothed to the King of Cornwall.
Laurence Sterne (1713-1768) wrote *Tristram Shandy*, a humorous
novel.
Other form: **Tristan** (Welsh, German, French).

Trixie familiar form of **Beatrix**.

Troy (f)
From the surname, itself from the name of the French city of Troyes.

Trudi familiar form of **Gertrude**.

Trudie familiar form of **Gertrude**.

Trudy familiar form of **Gertrude**.

Tudor anglicized form of Welsh **Tudur**.

Tudur (m)
From Welsh meaning 'people' + 'ruler'. A popular traditional name
in Wales and the borders of Wales.
Other forms: **Tudor** (anglicized), **Tudyr** (older Welsh spelling).

Tyrone (m)
From the Irish place name County Tyrone, meaning 'Owen's
Country'. The actors Tyrone Power and his son of the same name
made it well-known in the first half of the 20th century.

Una (f)
From Irish Gaelic **Úna**, of uncertain origin, but frequently considered
to be a female form of the Latin for 'one'. Una Stubbs is a modern
stage and television actress.
Variant forms: **Oona, Oonagh.**
Familiar form: **Oonie.**

Unice variant form of **Eunice**.

Unity (f)
From the word unity. Unity Mitford, sister of the writer Nancy Mitford, was a 20th- century bearer of this name.

Urban (m)
From Latin meaning 'of the city'. Several popes bore this name but it is uncommon in modern times.

Ursula (f)
From Latin meaning 'little she-bear'. St Ursula was a 4th-century martyr whose life story is obscured by myth. She is said to have been one of 11,000 virgins who were put to death by the Huns in Cologne because Ursula refused to marry their chief. Ursula Andress is a fim star.

Val familiar form of **Valentine,Valerie**.

Valary variant form of **Valerie**.

Valda (f)
An invented name which has appeared in the 20th century.

Valentine (m)
From Latin meaning 'healthy'.
Familiar form: **Val.**

Valerie (f)
French, from Latin **Valeria** derived from the Roman family name from a Latin word meaning 'to be strong'. St Valeria was an early Christian saint.
Variant form: **Valarie, Valery.**
Familiar form: **Val.**

Van (m)
Of uncertain origin, possibly from the surname **Vance** meaning 'fen-dweller' or from a familiar form of **Ivan**. Van Morrison is a world famous singer/songwriter.

Vance (m)
From the surname, itself from Old English meaning 'fen-dweller'.

Vanda variant form of **Wanda** which reflects the German pronunciation.

Vanessa (f)
Invented by Jonathan Swift (1667-1745) for his friend Esther Vanhomrigh, from elements of her first name and surname. It has caught parents' fancy this century, perhaps as a result of Hugh Walpole's novel *Vanessa* (1933) and the fame of actress Vanessa Redgrave.
Familiar form: **Nessa**.

Varda (f)
From Hebrew meaning 'rose'.

Vaughan (m)
From Welsh meaning 'little'. Outstanding as the name of the composer Ralph Vaughan Williams (1872-1958).

Vera (f)
From Latin, meaning 'true'. Not so much used recently as at the start of the 20th century, but a household name because of Vera Lynn, a singer who inspired the troops during World War II.

Verena (f)
Of uncertain origin. St Verena was a 3rd-century Swiss saint.

Verity (f)
From the word meaning 'truth', much used by the Puritans in the 17th century.

Verna (f)
Of uncertain origin, but perhaps a female form of **Vernon**, or from Latin meaning 'spring'.

Vernon (m)
From the surname, itself based on a French place name, meaning 'alder tree'.

Veronica (f)
From Latin, meaning 'true image', the term used for the cloth which
was imprinted with the features of Jesus after he wiped his face with
it. The compassionate woman who offered it has always been revered
as St Veronica, though her real name is not known. The flower
veronica probably takes its name from the saint.

Vi familiar form of **Violet.**

Vic familiar form of **Victor, Victoria.**

Vickie familiar form of **Victoria.**

Vicky familiar form of **Victoria.**

Victor (m)
From Latin, meaning 'conqueror'. Popular through the ages as the
name of martyrs, popes and modern film stars.
Familiar forms: **Vic.**

Victoria (f)
Female form of **Victor.** Its popularity was enhanced when Queen
Victoria came to the throne in 1837.
Familiar forms: **Vic, Vickie, Vicky, Tory, Vikki, Viki, Vita.**

Viki familiar form of **Victoria.**

Vikki familiar form of **Victoria.**

Vin familiar form of **Vincent.**

Vince (m)
Familiar form of **Vincent,** used as a name in its own right.

Vincent (m)
From Latin, meaning 'conquering'. It is the name of many saints,
including Vincent de Paul, 16th-century French missionary and
helper of the poor. The artist Vincent van Gogh was a modern bearer

of the name, along with the actor Vincent Price and the footballer
Vinnie Jones.
Familiar form: **Vince, Vin, Vinnie, Vinny.**

Vinnie, Vinny familiar forms of **Lavinia,Vincent** or **Virginia.**

Viola (f)
From Latin meaning 'violet'. In Shakespeare's *Twelfth Night*, Viola ,
disguised as a man, causes much confusion, but eventually marries
Duke Orsino.

Violet (f)
The flower name used as a first name. Like many flower names, it
was well-used until the 1920s in Britain.
Familiar form: **Vi.**

Virginia (f)
From the female form of the Roman family name **Verginius.** The
spelling **Virginia,** adopted in the 4th century, suggests that it was
considered to be from the Latin word for 'virgin'. For this reason,
Elizabeth I of England was hailed by poets as Virginia, the Virgin
Queen and the American state was named in her honour. Virginia
Bottomley , a cabinet minister of the 1990s, is a modern bearer of the
name.
Familiar forms: **Ginny, Ginnie, Jinny, Vinny, Vinnie.**

Vita (f)
Either a female form of **Vitus,** 4th-century patron saint of sufferers
from nervous disorders, or a short form of **Victoria,** as in the case of
the writer Vita Sackville West (1892-1962).

Viv familiar form of **Vivian** or **Vivien.**

Vivian (m and f)
From the Roman family name **Vivianus,** probably derived from the
Latin word meaning 'living'. In this spelling it is nearly always male.
Familiar form: **Viv.**

Vivien (f and m)
From the Roman family name **Vivianus,** probably derived from the

Latin word for 'living'. In this spelling it is nearly always female, which explains why the 20th-century actress Vivien Leigh changed the original form of her first name, Vivian, to Vivien,
Other form: **Vivienne.**
Familiar form: **Viv.**

Wade (m)
From the surname, itself based on the place name meaning 'ford'.

Waldo (m)
From the German name **Waldemar** meaning 'power'. Ralph Waldo Emerson (1803-1882) was an American writer and philosopher.

Wallace (m)
From the Scottish surname, itself meaning 'Welshman'. Sir William Wallace (1274-1305) fought for Scottish independence against Edward I of England. Despite many victories, he was eventually captured and executed. See also **Wallis.**

Wallis (f and m)
Variant form of **Wallace**, uncommon apart from the famous example of Wallis Simpson, who married the Duke of Windsor in 1937 and, as a divorced woman, provoked a constitutional crisis.
Familiar form: **Wally.**

Wally familiar form of **Wallace, Walter.**

Walt (m)
Familiar form of **Walter**, used as a name in its own right by Walt Disney (1901-1966) maker of films and cartoons.

Walter (m)
From Germanic, meaning 'ruling people'. Less used now than at the start of the 20th century.
Familiar forms: **Wally, Walt, Wat, Wattie** (last two Scottish).

Wanda (f)
Of uncertain origin, but perhaps from a Slavonic tribal name. Fairly common in Eastern Europe, it appeared at the end of the 19th century in Britain. *A Fish called Wanda* is the title of a recent film.

Variant form: **Vanda.**

Warren (m)
From the surname, itself of Norman-French origin from the place name, meaning 'game park'. Warren Hastings (1732-1818) was a British Governor of Bengal. Warren Beatty is a well-known American actor.

Wat Scottish familiar form of **Walter.**

Wattie Scottish familiar form of **Walter.**

Wayne (m)
From the surname meaning 'carter' or 'maker of carts'. Wayne Sleep is a well-known 20th-century dancer.

Webster (m)
From the surname meaning 'weaver'. Webster Booth was an early 20th-century singer.

Wenda variant form of **Wendy.**

Wendoline variant form of **Gwendolyn.**

Wendy (f)
Invented by J M Barrie for the 'little mother' in his play *Peter Pan*. A child acquaintance used to refer to the playwright as her 'friendy-wendy' and so the name was born.
Variant form: **Wenda.**

Wesley (m)
From the surname, itself from a place name meaning 'west meadow'. John Wesley (1703-1791) founder of the Methodist Church, made this an obvious choice for Methodists, but it is now used more widely, especially among West Indians. Wesley Snipes is an American actor.

Whitney (f)
From the surname, itself from the place name meaning 'white island'. Whitney Houston is the name of a 20th-century singer.

Wilbur (m)
Of uncertain origin, possibly from the surname **Wildbore**. Wilbur
Wright (1867-1912) was an American aviation pioneer.

Wilf familiar form of **Wilfred**.

Wilfrid (m)
From Germanic meaning 'will' + 'peace'. St Wilfred was an 8th-
century bishop of York.
Familiar form: **Wilf**.

Wilhelmina (f) [willa-mee-na]
Female form of the German name **Wilhelm**, meaning 'will' +
'protection'. Rarely used.
Familiar form: **Wilma**, used as a name in its own right and much
preferred to the original.

Will familiar form of **William**.

Willa (f)
Originally a female form of **William**, now used as a name in its own
right. Willa Cather (1876-1947) was an American poet and novelist.

William (m)
Norman-French of Germanic origin, meaning 'will' + 'protection'.
William the Conqueror introduced it to England in 1066 and it has
had lasting popularity ever since. Several kings have borne the name
and the elder son of Prince Charles is also William.
Other forms: **Uilleam** [ool-yam] (Scottish Gaelic), **Uilliam, Liam**
(both Irish Gaelic),**Gwilim, Gwilym, Gwyllim** (Welsh).
Familiar forms: **Bill, Billie, Billy, Will, Willie, Willy**.

Wilma familiar form of **Wilhelmina**.

Wilmer (m)
Of uncertain origin, possibly from Germanic meaning 'desire' +
'famous', but more probably a male form of **Wilma**.

Win familiar form of **Winifred**.

Windsor (m)
From the surname, itself based on a place name meaning 'river bank with a winch for hauling boats'. Despite being the surname of the royal family it is not a popular first name.

Winifred (f)
From Welsh, meaning 'blessed reconciliation' and merged with an Old English name meaning 'joy' + 'peace', eventually taking on its present spelling. St Winifred was a 7th-century Welsh saint, still commemorated at Holywell, North Wales. She was beheaded by a Prince whose advances she rejected and where her head fell, a spring (the holy well) gushed forth.
Familiar form: **Win, Winn,Winnie, Freda.**

Winston (m)
From a surname, itself from a place name, meaning 'Win's place'. First name of Winston Leonard Spencer Churchill, British statesman (1874-1965). West Indians favour it as a first name.

Wolf (m)
Perhaps a short form of the German **Wolfgang,** or a name in its own right after the name of the animal. Mainly used by Jews.

Woodrow (m)
From the surname, itself from a place name suggesting a row of dwellings near a wood. Thomas Woodrow Wilson (1856-1924) was 28th president of the USA and Woodrow Wyatt a 20th-century British politician and journalist.
Familiar form: **Woody.**

Woody (m)
Perhaps a short form of **Woodrow,** or a nickname in origin, from the surname **Woods.** Not uncommon in the 20th-century entertainment world, as in Woody Allen, Woody Guthrie and Woody Herman.

Wynne (m)
From Welsh, meaning 'white, fair'. Common in Wales. Also a variant form of **Gwyn.**
Variant form: **Wyn.**

Xanthe (f) [zanth-ee]
From Greek meaning 'yellow' + 'bright'.

Xavier (m) [zay-vee-er]
From the surname of the 17th-century Spanish saint, Francis Xavier, itself a Basque place name meaning 'new house'.

Xenia (f) [zen-ya]
From Greek, meaning 'hospitable'. Rarely used in this original form. See **Zena**.

Yasmin variant form of **Jasmine.** Yasmin le Bon is a famous model of the 1990s.

Yasmine variant form of **Jasmine.**

Yehuda see **Jude.**

Yehudi (m)
From Hebrew meaning 'Jew'. Since his infancy (as a child prodigy violinist), Yehudi Munuhin has made the name well-known. See also **Jude.**

Yola familiar form of **Yolande.**

Yolanda variant form of **Yolande.**

Yolande (f)
From French, of Greek origin, meaning 'violet flower'. It is an adaptation of **Iolanthe,** now only known from the opera by Gilbert and Sullivan (1882) about a fairy who marries a mortal. Another operatic association is the heroine of Tchaikovsky's *Yolanta* (Provençal spelling) about a blind girl who regains her sight when she falls in love.
Variant form: **Yolanda.**
Familiar form: **Yola.**

Yves see **Yvette, Yvonne.**

Yvette (f) [ee-vet]
From Old French, meaning 'yew bow'. It is the female form of **Yves**, which has never been used as a British name. See **Yvonne**.

Yvonne (f)
From Old French , meaning 'yew bow'. Like **Yvette**, it is a female form of the male French name **Yves**, but to a much greater extent than **Yvette**, it has been used widely as an independent name in the English-speaking world.
Variant form: **Evonne**.

Zachariah (m)
Biblical from Hebrew, meaning 'Jehovah has remembered'.
Zachariah in the New Testament is the father of John the Baptist and was struck dumb for showing a lack of faith (Luke 1). Since the 18th century, uncommon in this form.
Variant form: **Zachary**.
Familiar form: **Zak**, used as a name in its own right by the Beatle, Ringo Starr, for his son.

Zana familiar form of **Susannah**.

Zandra (f)
Familiar form of **Alexandra**, used as a name in its own right, as in the name of the designer of exotic fashions, Zandra Rhodes (1940-).

Zane (m)
From a surname, itself possibly a place name, or a Danish form of John. Zane Grey (1875-1939) was born in Zanesville, a town founded by one of his ancestors.

Zara (f)
From Arabic, meaning 'splendour', or 'flower', but also taken to be a variant form of **Sarah**, meaning 'princess'. In literature and life it has royal associations. Zara is the African Queen in Congreve's
Mourning Bride (1697) and Princess Anne's daughter is Zara Phillips.

Zelda (f)
Of uncertain origin, but as used by British and American Jews it is

likely to be an English form of the Yiddish **Zelde**, meaning 'happiness'. It can also be a familiar form of **Griselda**.

Zelma (f)
Originally a familiar form of **Anselma**, itself a female form of **Anselm**, used as a name in its own right.

Zena (f)
Of uncertain origin, but probably both a familiar form of names ending in -*ina*, and possibly a variant form of **Xenia**.

Zenobia (f)
From Greek meaning 'power of Zeus'.

Zephania (f) [zef-an-eye-a]
Biblical, from Hebrew meaning 'Jehovah protects'. In the Old Testament, it is the name of a book called after a minor prophet.

Zeta variant form of **Zita**.

Zilla variant form of **Zillah**.

Zillah (f)
Biblical, from Hebrew, meaning 'shadow'. Common up to the late 19th century.
Variant form: **Zilla**.

Zinnia (f)
From the name of a colourful daisy-like flower.

Zita (f)
From an Italian dialect word meaning 'girl'. St Zita was the 13th-century patron saint of Lucca in Tuscany and of servants, as she was in domestic service.
Variant form: **Zeta**.

Zoë (f) [zo-ee]
From Greek, meaning 'life'. St Zoe was an early martyr.
Variant form: **Zoey**.

Zola (f)
Of uncertain origin, perhaps from the Italian surname Zola. The runner Zola Budd has made this unusual name well-known in modern times.